MAID MA

'A wind's in the heart of me, a fire's in my heels,
I am tired of brick and stones and rumbling wagon-wheels,
I hunger for the sea's edge, the limits of the land,
Where the wild old Atlantic is shouting on the sand.'

A Wanderer's Song, John Masefield

SOUTHAMPTON WATER, THE SOLENT AND SPITHEAD 1944

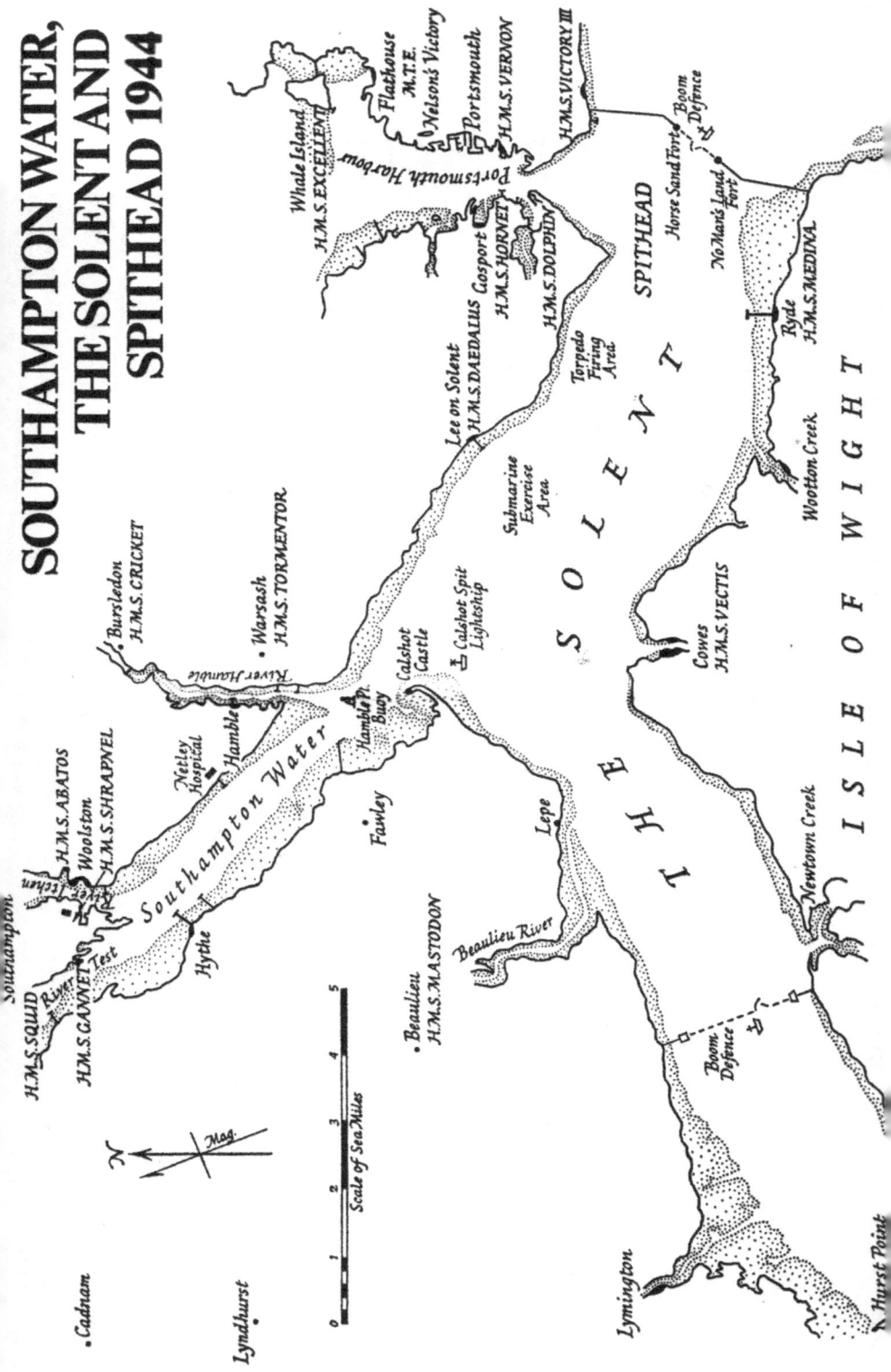

Flathouse
M.T.E.
Nelson's Victory
Portsmouth
H.M.S. VERNON
H.M.S. VICTORY III

Whale Island
H.M.S. EXCELLENT

Portsmouth Harbour

Gosport
H.M.S. DAEDALUS
H.M.S. HORNET
H.M.S. DOLPHIN

Horse Sand Fort
Boom Defence

No Man's Land Fort

Ryde
H.M.S. MEDINA

Lee on Solent

SPITHEAD

Torpedo Firing Area

Submarine Exercise Area

Wootton Creek

S O L E N T

Bursledon
H.M.S. CRICKET

Warsash
H.M.S. TORMENTOR

River Hamble

Cowes
H.M.S. VECTIS

T H E

Netley Hospital

Hamble

Hamble Buoy

Calshot Castle

Calshot Spit Lightship

I S L E   O F   W I G H T

H.M.S. ABATOS
Woolston
H.M.S. SHRAPNEL

Fawley

Lepe

Newtown Creek

Southampton

River Itchen

H.M.S. SQUID
H.M.S. GANNET
River Test

Hythe

Southampton Water

Beaulieu
H.M.S. MASTODON

Beaulieu River

Boom Defence

• Cadnam

N

Mag.

5
4
3
2
1
0
Scale of Sea Miles

Lyndhurst

Lymington

Hurst Point

MAID MATELOT
The Adventures of a Wren Stoker in World War Two

ROZELLE RAYNES

First published in 1971 by the Nautical Publishing Company

Second edition published in 1993 by Warsash Publishing

Third edition published in 2004 by Castweasel Publishing

Fourth edition published in 2022 by Golden Duck (UK) Ltd
Sokens, Green Street, Pleshey, nr Chelmsford, Essex, CM3 1HT
golden-duck.co.uk

Front cover: *Girl with a Cat (Lady Rozelle)* by Countess Manvers,
from the Pierrepont Collection,
reproduced by kind permission of the Earl Manvers Will Trust

A CIP catalogue record for this book is available from the British
Library.

ISBN 978-1-899262-51-9

Printed and bound in the UK by Biddles Books Ltd
biddles.co.uk

Contents

Foreword

MAID MATELOT is a shout for freedom, written from page one to put distance between Rozelle Raynes and her parents, their status and their estates. Her father, Captain The Hon. Gervas Pierrepont MC, was a gloomy man married to Marie Louise Butterfield, daughter of a Keighley worsted manufacturer, who was much looking forward to becoming Countess Manvers after the death of her husband's mad, unmarried cousin. Most of the considerable Butterfield fortune had descended on Marie Louise so her third child, christened Frederica, started life with the comfortable prospects of the younger daughter of an earl and next to no responsibility or expectation.

Lady Rozelle.

Then her brother, Evelyn, born to be 7th Earl Manvers, died of scarlet fever and Venetia, her older sister, died of septicaemia after a tonsil extraction. Suddenly the gentle, blonde and very pretty five-year-old Ricky was the cynosure of every eye. She went from being a privileged nobody to being the sole heir to a noble household—the one everyone wanted a bit of.

Born in 1925, she was as awkward a fourteen-year-old as there could be when the second great war started and her father, at last, inherited. The family transferred to Thoresby, one of the three great estates in Nottinghamshire known as Dukeries, each a monstrous mansion full of precious chattels. In honour of their new style Ricky switched to using her second name and became 'Lady Rozelle'. The War Office requisitioned the house and sent the Warwickshire Yeomanry to occupy it and to cut up her father's park with their tanks and trenches.

By morning she went in the bus to the girl's grammar school in Mansfield and, in the evening, she came home to the riot of young officers using the great hall, at the heart of the house, as their mess. It was wonderfully exciting, but with reams of tragedy waiting to be written into the later episodes.

The conflict wore on and the soldiers, hearty and happy in training, were deployed to North Africa and elsewhere. The attrition rate among the subalterns, who had paid gracious court to the blonde heiress, was grisly.

Rozelle wanted out, in part to escape the lifelong expectations imposed by her inheritance and, more so, by the sense that she must do her duty for her country. Thoresby lies as far from the sea as you can get in England and, 'seething with a desperate longing to get older as fast as possible,' the Women's Royal Navy Service became her escape hatch.

At the Drafting Depot in Mill Hill the privilege of hitherto was shaken out of her by the need to manage her own affairs, when even putting sheets on her bunk was a challenge. But entranced by the strangeness of everything and by the new friends she was able to make, she took to the service with gusto and a satisfaction she was never able to replicate in her life after the war. She writes each stage of basic training, and then deployment, in the breathless style of a young girl's diary. But the WRNS, which advertised itself with the tag line 'Join the Wrens and free a man for the fleet', subjected her to a series of interviews on which of the approved tasks for women she should be trained for. She was desperate to be a Boats' Crew Wren, in preference to typing the, admittedly vital, reports from Bletchley Park, or being the radio mechanic on an aircraft. She managed this by being alternately dumb and clever and after an extended five interviews she was trained as a boat's motor mechanic or, in Navy speech, a stoker.

She loved the life. The more cold and wet she was, the more chapped and frozen her hands, the more she felt she was doing her bit. She might have ordered her uniform and blue Stoker's badges from Gieves' in Bond Street, but by now she felt wholly at ease out of her birth class, working alongside the Royal Navy and Wrens' ratings she drank beer and danced with. She stripped engines and rebuilt them; she scraped, caulked and re-painted hulls; she polished brass; she knew these inanimate objects better than anybody.

As she learned her way around Southampton Water as part of a team which kept the fleet going day and night, she also noticed a steady build-up of men and equipment, and a ratcheting up of general secrecy applied to the most mundane operations.

Through 1944 she found herself at the epicentre of the D-Day invasion fleet. Her small motor boats—and there were many—were in constant demand, carting men and material from shore to the ships of the largest invasion fleet ever assembled. Some of her boats worked well and earned her respect and love, some less so. One sank. Tension of a different kind comes into her writing when she tells of taking the men she knows to the landing craft, where they await the start flare for the 160-mile slog across the channel to the Normandy beaches.

She switches from the personal and affectionate style of the early chapters to give a succinct and clear recap of the high command decision making for the bridgehead into Europe. She makes a strong connection between the defining reasons for the delay of 24 hours to the planned start and what it felt like to the men locked on board tiny tin cans, bobbing about in the tidal mishmash of the Solent. The mix of observation and emotion captures the time and place perfectly and makes this book far more than the unexceptional diary of a teenager towards the end of the war.

She knew then, in the aftermath of invasion and eventual victory in Europe, and as the whole military establishment was demobbed, that her time in the Wrens would end soon. She did everything possible to deny the tide but, the 'numb misery' of ceasing to be a Wren Leading Stoker, and returning to a life of wealth and luxury, sickened her.

Her epilogue, written half a lifetime later, tells the career stories of the friends she made in those days and gives the clue to her love for the service as the perfect mix of comradeship and sea. Life was never as good again.

Hugh Matheson

18 March 2022

Rozelle.

Hugh Matheson was born a distant cousin of Rozelle Pierrepont and was without expectations when they were placed next to each other at a grand dinner. He had misunderstood the invitation and arrived late and scruffy. She was intrigued enough to question him closely on his laying bricks for a living in spite of having been at Oxford (briefly). A week later she asked his mother to invite him to take on her Thoresby inheritance, which had troubled her so much.

Her difficulties had begun when her brother Evelyn, who should have inherited by primo geniture, died of scarlet fever aged five. Her choice of Hugh Matheson carried the irony that because he was the youngest child of the youngest child of the earl Manvers who settled the estate, it was an inheritance by ultimo geniture.

Rozelle stayed away from Thoresby as much as she could and sailed, taught sailing, wrote about sailing, and was for many years reports secretary of the Royal Cruising Club. But, when she fell at 84 and broke several bones, Hugh persuaded her to live permanently in a house that she and her husband, Dick, had built by the river in the park. He was able to recruit a wonderful team of carers from close about who gave her unconditional love and support. Her suspicion of her wealth and the grandeur of the place, which encloses the last untouched bits of the ancient woodland of Sherwood, evaporated, and when she died four years later there was no longer a need to escape but a calm acceptance of her fate.

Hugh is a successful rower, sports coach, journalist and author. He competed in three Olympic Games, including being part of Britain's silver medal-winning team in Montreal 1976 and finishing in 6th place in the single sculls in Moscow in 1980.

Thoresby Hall.

Editor's Note

I WALKED INTO MY parents' bedroom one morning in 1969 to find my father clutching a bright yellow hardback among the usual chaos of newspapers, post and the remains of breakfast. This was Rozelle Raynes's first book *North in Nutshell*. I can't remember if he'd been sent it for review or as a gift from the author. I was 15 and not especially interested. What has stayed with me to this day was how honoured he felt by this friendship and how much he admired Lady Rozelle. This was a feeling shared by many yachtsmen of that time, though she was never a sailing celebrity. I'm grateful to Richard Woodman for contributing his personal appreciation and giving a sense of her personality to a new generation of readers.

North in a Nutshell was her first book, written with the confidence that had come from her happy second marriage to Dick Raynes in 1965. It describes a three-month exploration of the Norwegian coast in her much-loved *Martha McGilda*, a 25′ Folkboat with a Seagull outboard engine. It's adventurous and admirable but lacks the vital qualities of self-discovery and human observation which make *Maid Matelot* special. This, her second book, was written soon after *North in a Nutshell* using the diaries and letters of her teenage self and her insight as an adult into the person she'd been then—and the time in which she'd lived.

Hugh Matheson is absolutely right to describe *Maid Matelot* as a 'shout for freedom'. It's an emotional as well as a spatial freedom: she doesn't just 'run away to sea', but analyses the person she finds when she gets there. On the front cover of this edition we see Rozelle as painted by her mother: on the title page we show one of her drawings of herself. Teenage Rozelle, no longer part of a grand establishment with household staff, discovers she is someone who relishes hard manual work, is not afraid of the elements and responds with uncomplicated gratitude to the kindness of a hot cup of cocoa or a 'sippers' of rum.

She's emotional, humble, determined and observant. There are some beautiful and some poignant moments, such as the singing from the Welsh crew on the tug-boat *Chokka* being taken up across the fleet as they wait for D-Day, then her first sight of German prisoners 'under-fed, tired and ill-looking youths wearing the ragged remains of their uniforms'. They were accompanied by 'a mangy black mongrel' which was hustled away in a police van, 'the doors shut irrevocably behind him'. Impossible to read without a pang of emotion.

She also discovers that salt sea air is an absolute necessary to her and that taking the tiller of a small boat gives her a thrill like nothing else. It would take some time after her return home before she find ways to follow her vocation but her time in the Wrens had also given her lifelong friends who understood her need. She pasted their photographs into a two-inch thick, leather bound album, annotating them carefully, decorating the pages and interspersing them with coloured pictures and poetry of the sea. It's an eloquent artefact and we're grateful to the Stonebridge Trust for its loan. The photos reproduced here can't really begin to reproduce the impression of painstaking labour—and love—that's encapsulated in the original.

Hugh Matheson, Gregor Pierrepont and the Trustees of the Thoresby Settlement have been kindness personified in their unhesitating support of this new edition. I remain personally indebted to Richard Woodman and my father, George Jones, for sharing their admiration of the adult Rozelle as a valiant sailor, committed philanthropist and loyal friend.

Julia Jones

Sue, Winkle and me in the bows of the *Camel* at B Steps.

Sue and Winkle.

Author's Preface

I T WAS A black stormy winter's night, with the wind blowing great guns from the south-west and an anti-aircraft gun on the end of the Ocean Dock firing at a lone German raider somewhere up amongst the constellation of Orion. There was quite a sea running, with the wind against the tide, and clouds of solid spray burst across the bows of our boat from time to time, causing a rivulet of icy water to funnel off the rim of my tin helmet into a small persistent channel which found its way inside my oilskin collar and, eventually, down the back of my neck. I leant over my beloved charge, an old 4-cylinder Kelvin engine, to make sure that the pistons were still singing their rhythmic song despite the fury of the elements; and suddenly I realized that this was my ideal situation in life, something towards which I had felt a definite pull ever since my earliest childhood.

The following chapters were written with the help of hasty notes scribbled in a diary and heavily censored letters written to my parents between the ages of seventeen and nineteen. If they show a narrow and childish outlook on life in general and the future in particular, I hope the reader will bear patiently with me and try to recall, if he or she is old enough, how it felt to grow up in the middle of a world war.

I never remember feeling alarmed when the air-raid sirens sounded, nor missing such luxuries as meat, real eggs, chocolates or bananas; there was quite a festive feeling on the rare occasions when they occurred, but I did not regret their absence, and I was quite incapable of appreciating the pleasures of the pre-war world which my mother promised me would return in the future.

During the last three years of the war, no past or future ever existed in my juvenile conception. There was only time for the magnificent present, filled with the war and the sea and ships. And because I could not perceive, as older people could, any signs of a bright new world beyond that limited horizon, I must have caused much trouble and anxiety to my devoted parents.

A quarter of a century has passed since those days, and although I have now altered my views on many of the important things in life, one situation has never changed, and that is the mystic pull of salt water. In the lives of most people there is a constantly recurring element, perhaps because they are bound to it by some secret bonds; one person is always making speeches, another one travelling and a third sowing seeds in the earth. In my life the floating and navigating element recurs with a persistent frequency, and I am fortunate enough to have a husband who encourages this deplorable tendency!

Dick Raynes, Rozelle and Texel on board Martha McGilda (from North in a Nutshell*).*

I

Salt Water in my Veins

'**B**E SURE TO wear your woollen combinations as soon as the weather turns cold,' adjured my mother, her eyes bleak with anxiety as she surveyed the long line of girls forming into a queue outside the Regulating Office.

I blushed furiously and hinted that it was time for her to go. I was seventeen years old and had seldom left home before without my parents. But I felt no twinges of regret or incipient homesickness as I looked up at the vast building which was about to engulf me; only a premonition of enormous joy, an utterly selfish emotion which took no account of my mother's feelings. It was August 25th, 1943, and I had arrived at HMS *Pembroke III* to join the Women's Royal Naval Service.

The seed was first sown at the tender age of three. Suddenly I became aware, without any shadow of doubt, of what I wanted to do when I grew up. And this absurd idea just grew and grew, but never changed its essential substance as most childish whims are apt to do. I wanted to work on a boat in a busy port.

I lived with my parents in a tall Victorian house in London, SW7, up till the age of thirteen. It was a lonely childhood after my brother and sister died, and whenever I took a particular dislike to my governess, which happened with an alarming frequency, I would make plans to run away to sea. These were often encouraged by a girl called Jessie McNeil who worked in our house. She came from the little island of Barra in the Outer Hebrides, and every Wednesday, when my governess had her afternoon off, Jessie used to take me for a walk in Hyde Park or Kensington Gardens. She had a brother who had been on Scott's first expedition to the Antarctic, and her conversation was always spiced with the flavour of maritime adventure. Sometimes, at night, I would lie awake listening to the sound of ship's sirens on the Thames, of which I know of no other sound filled with such magic potentialities; but I lacked the courage and strength of purpose to put my plans into action.

In those days my seagoing experiences consisted of an annual voyage to and from Gibraltar or Tangier in a P&O liner, a holiday to West Africa and the Canary Islands in an old banana-ship called the TSS *Voltaire*, and a great deal of time spent in rowing a sliding-seat skiff on the Serpentine in Hyde Park. My father encouraged this form of activity as he did the rudiments of boxing for little girls, and the study of chess, bridge and cryptography; and he never refused me a shilling with which to hire a boat after my lessons were done. I think my mother had her reservations on the subject, but she held her peace and it was too early for her to gauge the far-reaching effects of this infantile taste for a waterborne existence.

When the war started in 1939, we left London and went to live in the heart of Sherwood Forest. After a few weeks of constant pestering and persuasion on my part, my parents agreed to let me go to Queen Elizabeth's Grammar School in the mining town of Mansfield, about twelve miles away from where we lived.

Many people look back on their school days with a total lack of affection, but to me it was a period of considerable enchantment. There were some five hundred children at the school at that time, but our numbers soon swelled to over a thousand when Southend High School was evacuated to Mansfield. For half of each day we did our lessons in the air-raid shelters, to allow the other half of the school to use the class-rooms. And it was there that I first began to revel in the mysteries of trigonometry, on account of the exciting navigational problems often encountered. At the age of fourteen I was ridiculously shy, self-conscious and backward in most subjects, but these drawbacks were soon minimized in the warm and friendly atmosphere of the industrial North.

At home I studied army map-reading, cryptography, German news bulletins and the war at sea. I cut out all the photographs I could find of naval actions during the first three years of the war, and stuck them, methodically, into a large photograph album. I saved up my pocket-money for over a year in order to buy a prismatic compass, and with this thrilling toy I would spend many happy hours on the summits of hills, taking bearings of distant objects and plotting courses across an ordnance survey map.

Every night, at the end of my prayers, I always entreated, 'Please God, let the war go on long enough for me to take part in it'; and then I would fall asleep and dream of some immensely important maritime venture, perhaps a landing at dead of night on an enemy-occupied coast, in which I played a part of great responsibility and heroism.

After two years at Mansfield I matriculated, and then the question arose as to what was to be done with me next. My mother often regretted that there was no chance of having me properly finished off in Paris or Switzerland on account of the war, but my father encouraged me in my private ambition to join the WRNS as soon as possible. He even wrote one or two letters on my behalf to formidable ladies of his acquaintance, who commanded vast establishments of uniformed females. The correspondence grew and grew, but they were all agreed on one point, that I was no use to them until I had reached the advanced age of seventeen.

My mother was kept in the dark about this highly important and secretive correspondence. She made a number of tentative inquiries on her own behalf about my joining the local land army. In the meantime I stayed on at school studying mathematics, geography, and Spanish, and seething with a desperate longing to get older as fast as possible.

We were on holiday at Lynton in North Devon when the letter came. The hotel porter delivered it to me at the breakfast-table, so there was no chance of hiding it. It was a moment of supreme family drama and tension, and also of considerable beastliness. My father knew that my calling-up papers were inside the envelope as he had contrived to arrange things for me; my mother suspected something of the sort and treated the letter with the same recoil of horror as if it contained a verminous reptile; and I was bursting with irrepressible excitement, but also feeling upset and apprehensive about the bomb-shell which would undoubtedly explode in our midst.

There were banks of fluffy grey clouds casting small dark shadows over the sad undulations of Exmoor, and a hint of rain borne in on the westerly wind. The affairs of men seemed puny and trivial amidst a landscape of such stark grandeur, and no one noticed that we finished our breakfast in silence.

*   *   *

The WRNS Drafting Depot at Mill Hill, or HMS *Pembroke III*, was originally built as the National Institute of Medical Research, where a great many animals were housed for experimental work in the laboratories. By the time I arrived there in 1943, it accommodated several thousand girls, mostly new recruits expected to do two weeks of provisional training to prove their suitability for service life, after which they were drafted to naval bases all over the country.

When my turn came to report at the Regulating Office, my mother finally left. She had a taxi waiting near the gate and I watched her hat silhouetted against the rear window as the driver accelerated along the Ridgeway at Mill Hill.

I gave my particulars in a tremulous voice to a stern-faced female of some standing. She wore broad tortoise-shell spectacles and had a blue anchor stitched on to the left sleeve of her jacket, which struck me as being most becoming. Then followed a medical examination which was outstanding as a search for fleas, lice and other interesting livestock, rather than a study of inherent congenital diseases.

Later on that evening I found myself in a large room, termed a 'cabin', with nineteen other girls. We were issued with bedding to cover twenty bunks arranged in tiers of two around the walls. At that point I began to feel rather immature and homesick, for I had never made a bed before in my life. I watched the others out of the corner of one eye, and making a great show of shaking out blankets and fluffing up pillows, I set to work with an air of competence which deceived no one. Before long, two girls who had already made a polished job of their own bunks, came to my assistance and they soon initiated me into the mysteries of hospital corners and how to arrange the smart naval bedspreads so that they would excite no undue comment from the officer doing daily rounds.

Our days at Mill Hill were long and busy. We used to get up at 5 am every day, sweep, polish or scrub the floors, called 'decks', until 7.30 am, then have breakfast. Afterwards we scrubbed out the latrine block and continued polishing decks for a further two or three hours. After lunch we did squad drill, which involved marching up and down The Ridgeway to the accompaniment of much merriment from the local children. Then followed several hours of lectures on naval etiquette, the system of watch-keeping, the division of the navy into commands and sub-commands, nautical nicknames, how to deal with various types of gas attacks, who to salute and when, moral behaviour and sex, and a number of other fascinating subjects.

On my original application to join the WRNS I had put 'radio-mechanic' as the category I was most interested in, as I had been told there was no hope of becoming a Boats' Crew Wren and my father said that I might as well learn something which would be useful after the war.

After a few days at Mill Hill I was summoned to an interview. It only took the examiner a couple of minutes to discover that I would be quite unsuitable as a radio-mechanic, owing to my poor eyesight and dislike of flying. Next followed an interview for some exceedingly hush-hush concern called 'Ps' which took place, underground, somewhere in the heart of Bedfordshire. I had been forewarned by an old hand at Mill Hill, and soon managed to prove that I suffered from claustrophobia as well as eye-strain.

Interview followed interview with a monotonous regularity. An average one usually followed along these lines:

Interviewer—'Good morning, Wren P. I understand you would like to become a Wren Torpedoman?'

Me—'Good morning, Ma'am. I never said that I wanted to be one, but Second Officer G suggested it.'

Interviewer—'What did you learn at school which would be helpful in this particular category?'

Me—'Nothing, Ma'am. My best subjects were Trigonometry, Geography and Languages.'

Interviewer—'Do you realize that this is the fifth interview you have had and it is only on account of your age that given any choice in the matter at all? If you had been conscripted you would have had to take the first job that was offered to you.'

Me—'Yes, Ma'am. But I really wanted to work on a boat more than anything else, ever since I was three.' (At this point my eyelids would swell up and turn red, and I usually had to blow my nose vigorously!)

Interviewer—'You really are an utterly hopeless case, Wren P. Dismiss.'

The authorities began to get tired of trying to fit a square peg into a round hole. One glorious morning I was sent for and told that one of the first Wren Stoker's courses was due to start in Portsmouth shortly, and I should be drafted there the following Wednesday. I felt quite weak with jubilation and made but a poor show of expressing my thanks.

The next day I received my kit. Besides the usual WRNS uniform it included two pairs of bell-bottomed trousers, two seaman's square-necked blouses, a very thick navy-blue jersey, several pairs of 'blackouts' (heavy woollen knickers, also in navy-blue), a white lanyard and a most ferocious-looking knife with a sharp-pointed implement on one side of it which I learned was called a marline-spike.

One evening my father came to Mill Hill to take me out to dinner at a local restaurant called the Hunter's Horn. I remember having difficulty in swallowing my food because I was so puffed up with pride and excitement, showing off my new uniform to him and the marvellous weapon which could be attached to a canvas belt round one's waist.

My last few days at Mill Hill were rather an anticlimax. I had changed from a Pro-Wren into a fully fledged Wren; I knew how to salute smartly and had an official number, 65152, engraved with my name on an identity disc which hung round my neck. Indubitably I was ready to join the first draft to Portsmouth, to the world of those who go down to the sea in ships which I had always longed for.

On Tuesday morning my name was included in a list of girls to leave the following day for the WRNS Drafting Depot at Southsea. By lunch-time I had lost my voice completely and could only utter a few husky unintelligible noises. I was sent to the sick-bay and kept there for several days, whilst my draft left for Southsea.

For some obscure reason it was only possible to travel to Portsmouth on a Wednesday from HMS *Pembroke III*. By the week-end I had regained my voice and was put on light duties in the galley and the carpenter's shop, where the identity discs were made. Never have I known a week to creep by so slowly!

Maggie doing semaphore from *Anndora's* bows.

Tim bearing off with the boathook up for'ard.

2

Learning to be a Stoker

PORTSMOUTH, SEPTEMBER 1943: A town of gaping craters and mountains of rubble under a clear blue sky filled with silver balloons; a town teeming with naval uniforms, the secret movements of shipping, pubs filled with raucous voices singing their hearts out, and never-ending rumours about the Second Front.

I was met by a Leading Wren at the town station and driven briskly across the centre of Portsmouth and Southsea to Pendragon, a small private hotel overlooking Clarence Parade, which had been converted into the WRNS Drafting Depot. It was a very different set-up from the huge friendly depot at Mill Hill. There was a Chief Petty Officer in charge, and she was reputed to have run a girls' Borstal before the war. Pendragon, or HMS *Victory III*, was run on similar lines.

I had two or three weeks to wait before my course was due to start and the days passed rather slowly scrubbing decks, cleaning windows, known as 'portholes', washing dishes, doing squad drill along the sea front and attending lectures, all under the strict supervision of our Chief Petty Officer.

I used to enjoy scrubbing the front door steps of Pendragon best of all as one could usually pause from time to time to gossip with the postman or milkman doing their morning rounds. As long as the front door remained closed and no indignant faces appeared at any of the windows, our conversation would flow with a pleasant familiarity:

'Whatcher, Blondie! You ain't done much scrubbin' by the looks of them steps!'

'Well they won't look much better if you plant your big hooves all over them!'

'You shut yer trap! Ow's the ole cow this mornin'?'

'Doesn't change. Gave one of the girls Number Elevenses yesterday for coming in two minutes after 10 pm.'

'Aughta give 'em to you too, the way you done them steps! Ta ta, Blondie; see you temorrer.'

One morning another girl and I, under the charge of a Petty Officer, were ordered to march to Coronation House, the WRNS Headquarters some two miles away in the centre of Portsmouth. On arrival there we swept and dusted the Wren Superintendent's private office, which took us about twenty minutes, then marched back to Pendragon in time for breakfast. This outing was considered a great honour.

But life was not all hard work. From our cabin windows there was a never-ending pageant of shipping to watch, which filled me with a mixture of awe and excitement. I had seen plenty of photographs of destroyers, corvettes, minesweepers, submarines and MTBs before; in fact my album at home was full of them. But never in my life had I seen them in the flesh, so to speak, actually steaming across my field of vision at all hours of the day and night.

It was not surprising that many of our lectures dealt with security and keeping our mouths firmly shut when amongst strangers, and all our letters were heavily censored.

One afternoon when we were off duty, two other girls and I went to Hayling Island and walked for miles across the desolate mud-flats in the fading autumn light. On our return to the western end of the island we made the alarming discovery that the last ferry back to Portsmouth had just left. There were two sailors idling in an aged motor-boat alongside the jetty, and we had to use all our powers of persuasion to get them to run us across to Eastney. The muddy condition of our shoes on our return to Pendragon, and the fact that I inadvertently allowed a trail of chips to escape from a hot parcel of fish and chips concealed under my jacket, left a very unfavourable impression on our Chief Petty Officer.

It was, therefore, not a moment too soon when my name appeared on the drafting board to go to HMS *Hornet* at Gosport the following Wednesday. I felt disappointed to be missing the Wren Stoker's course, but, on the other hand, thrilled and delighted to be getting a job on a boat so soon; and at the famous MTB base which, at that time, was commanded by Peter Scott.

I crossed Portsmouth Harbour on the ferry to Gosport and reported at the Regulating Office of HMS *Hornet*, bursting with all the pride and assurance of extreme youth. It only took a matter of three or four hours to prick my glorious bubble.

The Petty Officer in charge examined my papers and informed me that I had been drafted to *Hornet* as a deck-hand, for which job perfect eyesight was required; she would, therefore, arrange for me to have an eye test that afternoon. As soon as her back was turned I removed my glasses and hid them in my suitcase, vowing that I would never wear them again.

A Boats' Crew Wren came to fetch me before long, and showed me all around the base. There were rows of glistening grey MTBs moored alongside the jetties, some with deep throbbing engines warming up like the heartbeats of monstrous leviathans. The Wrens' boats were large open cutters and pinnaces, all beautifully cared for and ready for instant use. The whole place was fairly humming with activity, and an air of feverish expectancy pervaded the peaceful afternoon. I could hardly believe my luck at having been sent to such a place.

Before long I was taken to the MO's office and left in an adjacent waiting-room whilst a search was being made for the man who was to test my eyes. I crept into the room next door, hastily copied all the letters on the testing screen on to a scrap of lavatory paper which I had secreted in my gas-mask container, returned to the waiting-room with the stealth of a burglar and learnt most of the letters off by heart. The occulist arrived in due course, did a thorough test of my eyes, looked sceptical, but was unable to prove that I was short-sighted. I left his office filled with a great surge of excitement as I felt that all my troubles had been finally overcome.

The Petty Officer with whom I had first spoken that afternoon then suggested to one of the coxswains that she might care to take me for a trial run. This entailed climbing over four other boats to reach the outermost one, and as there was a stiff breeze blowing, the boats were moving up and down in the most alarming manner. I glared enviously at the coxswain as she leapt nimbly from one gunwale to the next, whilst I was struggling desperately across the unfamiliar craft, trying to straddle two gunwales at a time, each moving in opposite directions.

At last I reached the ultimate boat; the coxswain had already started the engine and she ran across the thwarts, letting go first the bow-line then the stern-line, after which she thrust off from the other boats with a long boat-hook; all these tasks she accomplished in a matter of a few seconds.

I looked back at the receding shoreline of HMS *Hornet* and a certain premonitory twinge of apprehension rippled through my veins. The Petty Officer had been watching us all the time from the window of her office.

We circled the middle of Portsmouth Harbour once or twice, and the coxswain pointed out a number of interesting sights. There was HMS *Dolphin*, the submarine base, then we passed close to the famous gunnery school on Whale Island, HMS *Excellent*. After that we motored across to see the Foudroyant, a French sailing vessel which was captured by one of Nelson's ships at the Battle of Trafalgar and was reputed to be the oldest ship afloat.

I peered anxiously at these celebrated landmarks, but without my glasses they seemed to dance before my eyes in a bleary haze.

In the meantime the coxswain explained some of my duties as a deck-hand, and she said that I must always be ready to jump ashore with the bow-line when our boat was coming alongside, or to hold on to the jetty or ship's side with the boat-hook if it was only to be a short stop.

As we approached the landing-stage at HMS *Hornet*, she indicated that there was no time like the present and I had better go up for'ard and gather up the bow-line in readiness for mooring the boat. It was quite an ordeal crossing the five thwarts, as I did not yet feel inclined to hop from one to the other as the coxswain had done. Making about the same amount of commotion as a buffalo in a rowing-boat, I finally reached the bows and grabbed a piece of rope which was attached to a small bollard. The familiar outline of HMS *Hornet* loomed ahead of us, and I dimly perceived a group of sailors standing on the jetty beside a pile of heavy gear. I struggled up on to the small platform enclosing the sharp end of the boat and crouched there, like a winged hippopotamus. The coxswain shouted above the noise of the engine, 'Get ready to jump.' But I was expecting her to shout 'Jump', so I took off at the very first word of command. We were then about four yards away from the jetty but the distance meant nothing to me in that tense moment of decisive action!

There was an impressive displacement of water as I sank from sight; one of the sailors told me afterwards that he thought a torpedo had misfired!

The following sequence of events then took place in rapid succession. I was fished out of the water by a bearded Leading Seaman wielding a gigantic boat-hook which he attached to the seat of my bell-bottomed trousers; I was then hurried along to the Wrens' quarters to change my quarters to change my clothes and have a cup of tea; and, finally, I was seen off on the Gosport ferry, with a terse note returning me to the WRNS Drafting Depot at Pendragon.

Towards the end of September I went home on week-end leave. On my return I was sent to a house called Summerlands in Villiers Road, Southsea. There were only twenty Wrens living there, mostly engine-room ratings, and there was a very mild and agreeable Leading Wren in charge of us.

It was not long before I began to make friends with two girls who were both about five years older than me. One, Maureen Bolster, was tall and elegant with curly dark brown hair and vivacious golden-brown eyes, whilst the other, Margaret Boggis, was shorter with dark hair, intelligent green eyes and a smile of exceptional sweetness. Maureen had been a Factory Billeting Officer before she joined the WRNS, riding a motor-cycle all over Surrey in search of billets for the factory workers. She had a 'steady' Australian boy-friend in the RAF, and she regarded our introduction to naval life with reserve and discernment. Her father had been a Surgeon Captain in the Royal Navy.

Margaret Boggis was the daughter of a clergyman in South Devon, and she had achieved First Class Honours in Classics at Oxford before joining up. She hoped to become a school-teacher after the war.

For the next few months we three stayed together, and Maureen and Margaret took it upon themselves to shield me from the tougher aspects of service life. We developed a lasting friendship and agreed admirably on most subjects, but there was one point on which the other two were unable to sway my opinion, try as hard as they might; I had set out with a completely idealistic outlook on everything to do with the Royal Navy, and that was how it stayed. I turned a deaf ear to anyone who suggested that there were other ways of life and a few possible shortcomings in our present circumstances; for me it was the perfect existence, and thus it remained for the next two and a half years.

Soon after my arrival at Summerlands we started our Motor-Boat Driver's Course at the Mechanical Training Establishment in Portsmouth Dockyard. There were seven of us on the course, and we used to leave Southsea at 8.30 am every day and travel by bus to Flathouse, where we remained until 4 pm. It was a very happy month for all of us, and one which I often remembered with nostalgia in later years.

Our instructor was Chief Petty Officer Griffin, RN, a Warrant Officer of no mean stature. He was positively festooned with good conduct badges and long service stripes, and he reacted with philosophical resignation to the demands of modern times which permitted an influx of variegated females to invade the masculine stronghold of a ship's engine-room. He did not expect his class of Wren stokers to be endowed with much grey matter.

Our first week was devoted to the theory and principles of the Internal Combustion Engine. We wrote down copious notes about the functions of crankshafts, pistons, cylinders, carburettors, magnetos, etc., without really understanding anything much about it all. However, the notes included amusing coloured diagrams of a Circuit Rotating Magneto, a Delco-Remy Coil Ignition, the workings of a simple Jet Carburettor, and various other fascinating manoeuvres which were said to take place inside an engine. None of us doubted the enormous possibilities of the modern Internal Combustion Engine which Chiefie explained to us in such loving terms, and there was one sentence that he was fond of repeating which I shall remember till the end of my days.

'If you go dancing tonight, Girls,' he would say, and the band strikes up an old-time waltz; just you get on the floor and sing to yourselves these words to the tempo of the music—INDUCTION, COMPRESSION, POWER and EXHAUST'. (To illustrate his point Chiefie seized a leather cushion off his chair and waltzed it round the raised plaftorm on which his desk stood.) 'Never mind what your partner has to say, you just go on singing those words and you'll have the principles of the four-stroke engine fixed firmly in your pretty heads!'

We took his advice and started out on our dancing careers by attending a thé dansant at Kimballs, a highly respectable establishment in the heart of Southsea. Kimballs was a good place for a beginner, as one could always pretend one had come there solely for the purpose of having tea if nobody asked one to dance. We had not been there for more than a couple of minutes before Maureen was whisked away on the arm of a dashing Free French matelot. Margaret and I ordered tea, became engrossed in deep conversation and pretended that we didn't really mind that no one had asked us to dance.

A few days later we conceived a more daring plan. There was to be a dance in the pavilion on the end of South Parade Pier and we decided to attend this function. We had all scrubbed our lanyards until they shone like driven snow, and we were inordinately proud of these flimsy bits of rope as they distinguished us from the common herd as sea-going Wrens. Before setting off, Maureen gave us a short lecture on how to find a partner.

'Just choose a pillar near the entrance to the dance-hall,' she counselled us. 'And lean against it nonchalantly, as if you felt a little tired after too much dancing. Don't blush like a beetroot if anyone asks you to dance; just nod gravely and sail on to the dance floor with the calm assurance of a dowager duchess. And if you tread on his toes, DON'T EVER apologize!'

To begin with, our experience at Kimballs repeated itself. Maureen had hardly had time to select her pillar before she was invited to take the floor with a handsome Royal Marine. Margaret and I sat down close to our pillar and felt self-conscious and depressed. Obviously we lacked the magnetic charm which would cause men to abandon their drinks and fight each other for the honour of asking us to dance! We should probably be shunned like lepers the whole evening.

But in the end things turned out better than we had expected. Margaret and I both found ourselves on the dance floor, whirling round to the tune of a Viennese Waltz. My partner was a middle-aged Welsh sailor who said his name was Taffy; I did not know at that time that all Welshmen in the navy were called Taffy, just as all Liverpudlians were Scowse and all Irishmen Paddy.

In the middle of the dance I suddenly remembered Chiefie's injuctions and began to murmur Induction, Compression, Power and Exhaust in time with the rhythm of the waltz. Taffy asked me why I was making such a funny noise, then he himself burst into song, the pure lyrical music of the Welsh mountains. I listened enraptured, and promptly forgot all about the movements of the Internal Combustion Engine.

Later that evening Taffy escorted me back to Summerlands. It was the first proper dance I had ever been to and I felt immensely proud and grown up as I walked beside him along the sea front. We shook hands under a street-lamp in Villiers Road, and Taffy's parting words were: 'If you were my daughter I wouldn't never have let you join the WRNS.' My inflated ego exploded with the force of a thunderclap!

At the beginning of our second week on the course we were issued with boiler-suits and navy-blue kerchiefs, commonly known as sweat-rags. Then we were introduced to the engine workshops at Flathouse, which was an alarming experience.

Chiefie had instructed us on Monday morning about how to tie the sweat-rags round our hair so that no loose strands would escape from them; and he inspected our hands to make sure that we were not wearing any rings or bracelets.

'You could lose a couple of fingers in two shakes of a donkey's tail' he observed succinctly, if you go playing around with engines wearing them sort of female's baubles.'

I think this brought home to us the immensity and importance of our individual war efforts, more than any speeches by Winston Churchill on the BBC!

The workshops contained engines of every size and description, from the smallest two-strokes to the giant twelve-cylinder Rolls-Royce Merlin bomber engines. They also contained several hundred male stokers whose attention was riveted upon the seven extraordinary apparitions clad in brand new boiler-suits who were clustered round a small Diesel engine under the guardianship of a venerable Chief Petty Officer. The noise of the motors running was a solid wall of sound, and our nostrils were assailed by a strange mixture of petrol, Diesel oil, lubricating oil, melting grease and warm humanity. We could not hear a word that Chiefie was saying, and the vibrant roaring monster in front of us filled us with awe and dismay.

When eight bells struck for noon, we were allowed an hour's stand easy. There was usually a riotous stampede for the seamen's galley where we seized our plates of food, soon becoming adept at holding our own in the hungry jostling queue. After lunch, if there was any time left, we used to wander round the dockyard examining all the boats and ships with avid excitement, picturing ourselves at sea in sole charge of their engines in some desperate situation. At least that was what I used to do, but most of the others were more realistic and down to earth and their conversations would revolve round their homes, what they hoped to do after the war, boy-friends and civilian clothes.

There was one girl on our course who was quite different from all the others. Her name was Anne Norris and she came from a comfortable background. Her father and his brother owned a very old established family firm in the wine trade, and they lived in a fine large house in Surrey as well as having a holiday home in Cornwall and several yachts. Anne had fluffy blonde hair, always beautifully waved, vivid blue-grey eyes and a pink and white complexion which all contrived to give the effect of a rare and delicate piece of china, perhaps a Dresden shepherdess.

Almost everything about the WRNS was anathema to Anne. She saw no glamour in wearing a uniform, training to be a sea-going Wren and mixing with all classes of men and women. Her great interests in life were centred in her home and amongst her horses, which she loved and understood with a single-hearted devotion. However, in the Wrens' quarters Anne contrived to surround herself and her friends with an aura of comfort and homeliness, even in the bleakest and most unpromising of situations; but out on a boat she felt no inclination to prove how tough she was or to compete in the same job with a man. Sometimes Anne must have suffered for her point of view, as she was not a good mixer in a general sense but intensely loyal to the people that she counted as her friends. But whenever anyone was taken ill, no matter what the complaint, Anne came into her own. She always travelled with a suitcase full of remedies to fit all occasions, and her boundless sympathy and complete lack of spite towards anyone who had been unkind to her, made her a much sought-after nurse.

At the end of one week in the workshops most of us approached the smaller petrol and Diesel engines with a certain degree of confidence. We had learnt to handle our spanners with a knowing air, and we were capable of dismantling a carburettor and blowing ferociously through the jets, or removing the sparking-plugs, cleaning them and testing their gaps. The sight of our oil-ingrained finger-nails no longer disturbed us; in fact we were wont to exhibit our filthy hands with pride amongst the white-collared office-working Wrens whom we met in the evenings.

On Sunday mornings all traces of the Mechanical Training Establishment's workshops were obliterated with loving care, and our lanyards had been scrubbed to a dazzling whiteness before we joined the huge church parade of a hundred Wrens and two hundred sailors, marching behind the Royal Marine band. Sometimes we marched to the chapel at HMS *Excellent* on Whale Island, and at other times to Nelson's Victory, the flagship of the Portsmouth Command. But wherever the service took place, I was always deeply moved and impressed by the glorious martial music and the sound of such a mighty choir singing 'Eternal Father, Strong to Save'. The proud tradition of the Royal Navy seemed to embrace us all on these occasions.

During the last two weeks of our course we often went out in fast motor-boats on errands to various parts of Portsmouth Harbour. One afternoon we motored a long way up Fareham Creek, and each one of us was allowed to have a turn at steering the boat. The coxswain was an old Leading Seaman, his brown wrinkled face encrusted with the salt of a thousand voyages and his merry blue eyes filled with laughter as he watched our solemn expressions, absorbing all the buoys and beacons we passed as if our lives depended on them.

On the return journey the engine suddenly petered out and the boat was left drifting helplessly near the entrance to Portchester Creek. We soon discovered that she had run out of petrol, and there was nothing to be done until some other vessel appeared to offer us a tow.

It was very quiet out there in the fading light of an October afternoon, and the coxswain began to ask us about our homes to distract us from our cheerless situation. It transpired that he himself came from a small village called Bothamsall, only three miles away from where my parents lived in Sherwood Forest. He tried to pinpoint the exact position of my home and asked if I'd ever come across a geezer called M— who lived in a whacking great mansion in the middle of the forest. I mumbled something about having heard the name before, then hastily changed the subject for I could not bear the thought of him finding out that that was my father! My greatest wish was never to be known as anyone else but 65152 Wren Stoker Pierrepont whilst I was in the WRNS, and a dark cloud used to loom threateningly in a corner of my otherwise clear blue sky every time a murmur of my previous life and connections drifted into earshot. Perhaps it was because my father did not inherit all this grandeur until I was fourteen that I had such an irrepressible horror of all it implied. Anyway it was a great relief on that particular occasion when a large motor-launch appeared out of the gathering dusk and offered us a tow-rope. It was not long before we reached Asia

Pontoon and were sipping large mugs of tea laced with rum aboard our rescue ship.

As the date of our exam drew near, we all began to concentrate on our work with a desperate resolution born of the knowledge that if we failed we might be sent to join some other category, far away from boats and the sea.

The last afternoon was spent with Chiefie in the class-room, and he gave us an encouraging little talk followed by some rather special advice:

'If I were you, Girls,' he said. 'I shouldn't go out to the pictures or dancing tonight. Just you get along back home and look up a few points in your notebooks like the advantages of a Diesel engine over a petrol one, and the details of the lubricating system of a Thorneycroft engine; and you might even look up the uses of an anti-dribble valve, and perhaps work out a daily routine for the starting up, running and maintenance of a four-stroke engine. Don't think of them as cold bits of metal, Girls, but as human beings what's got to be fed and watered and cared for, same as you and me!'

We said goodnight to Chiefie and went straight back to our cabin at Summerlands, where we buried ourselves in our books for the rest of the evening.

Next morning the exam was due to start at 9 am Anne and I both approached our desks with gloomy forebodings and an unpleasant sinking sensation in the pits of our stomachs. Maureen, on the other hand, was a born optimist and wore a confident expression on her face, whilst Margaret looked peaceful and unharassed as usual, but no one really doubted that she would pass the exam for all her work was marked by a sort of quiet brilliance with which we could not hope to compete.

Chiefie smiled benignly down on us from his platform at the top of the class-room, and produced our exam papers out of a beige folder. I gazed anxiously at mine through spectacles which had suddenly become misty with fearful anticipation; but lo and behold! There were all our old friends about the lubricating system and the anti-dribble valve, etc., which Chiefie had recommended us to revise the previous evening. The only sound to be heard for the next four hours was the steady scratching of pen nibs on sheets of foolscap.

The results of the Second Wren Boat-Driver's Course were announced two days later. Maureen and Margaret had passed with more than 90% out of 100%, and the rest of us, with the exception of one girl, had all passed with over 70%.

We danced Chiefie round the class-room and took him out on the beer to celebrate that evening. Just before going to bed I wrote an urgent letter to my father asking him to buy me some blue Wren Stoker's badges at Gieves' in Bond Street. I posted it by express mail next morning.

Maureen, me, and Maggie.

Maggie, me, and Maureen in duffle coats on the slipway at *Abatos*.

3

Force Pluto

THE WEEKS FOLLOWING our exam were rather an anticlimax. We now considered ourselves fully fledged Second Class Stokers, ready and willing to tend the engines of any small vessel. We had blue propellers sewn on to the right sleeves of our jackets, and we were commonly referred to as 'Stokes' by all sailors; but it seemed that there were no boats short of a stoker just then and no one was anxious to employ us.

Every day we scrubbed and polished the decks at Summerlands until they shone like skating-rinks, and at night we often groped our way around Southsea in a thick black fog. Whenever there was an air-raid on, the great lorries which released this smoke screen would be abroad, filling the clean salt air with an indescribable mixture of choking opaque obscurity. Perhaps the German pilots found it as disconcerting as we did, for there were very few bombs dropped on Portsmouth during the autumn of 1943.

It was mid November before our drafts came through. One grey and frosty morning Maureen, Margaret and I found our names on the notice-board to go to HMS *Abatos* the following week. We were ready to explode with excitement, the more so because no one had ever heard of *Abatos* before, or knew where it was or anything about it. This added a touch of mystery to the glorious fact that we three had been chosen to go to a proper naval base at last, to do the job for which we had been trained.

On November 15th we travelled by train to Southampton and were met at the station by a Wren driver with a small van. She soon deposited us on the steps of the South-Western Hotel, which was then known as HMS *Shrapnel*. It was a huge forbidding Victorian pile overlooking the old docks, and the main part of the building was devoted to the training of electrical engineers. The Wren's quarters were on the top floor and they commanded an impressive view over the port. Our cabin was spacious, bathrooms were plentiful and there was central heating, but in other respects it was a dismal place to live in after Summerlands. And we soon discovered that the whole vast edifice was alive with cockroaches; we used to run races with them up the stairs at night, with small bets placed on the most lively-looking insects and a tempting morsel of cheese placed at the top of the staircase! After one or two unpleasant experiences on the first few mornings following our arrival, I always remembered to turn my shoes upside down at night, or put them on top of a cupboard out of reach of the indefatigable hordes.

But HMS *Shrapnel* was only where we slept at night, and the most important place in our lives soon became HMS *Abatos*, the naval base to which we had been assigned. It turned out to be an entirely new base in the suburb of Woolston, and we had to cross the River Itchen on a floating-bridge to get there. At that time the buildings were only half completed, and we gathered that it was to be the headquarters of Force Pluto, a highly secret organization in some way connected with the Second Front.

It was not until many months later that I learnt the meaning of PLUTO—*Pipe Line Under The Ocean*—and realized that it was a device for supplying fuel to the ships and armies on the coast of Normandy, after the first landings had taken place.

A number of ancient and rather battered cable-ships, trawlers and other small vessels were gradually acquired by Force Pluto. There was the *Holdfast, Latimer, Algeria* and *Persephone*. These were all cable-ships and the *Persephone* was known as the 'old yo-yo ship' as she always carried two immense rolls of pipe-line amidships, like the two halves of a yo-yo.

Then there were the trawlers *Lilac, Cedar* and *Coronia*, and the splendid deep-sea tugs *Bustler, Marauder* and *Samsonia*. We soon came to think of all these vessels as 'our ships', without, in the least, being aware of what they were up to.

There was a lonely spot called Lepe at the mouth of the Beaulieu River, and we often heard rumours about something very important in connection with Force Pluto, which was said to be taking place there, but no one who had been to Lepe would enlighten us on the subject.

On the day after our arrival in Southampton, six of us Wrens were sent to Hamble to fetch a fast motor-launch called *Anndora II* from a boat-building yard near by. Our coxswain was a Leading Seaman, Fred Clarke, who had been on the convoys to Murmansk for some while and was now due for a shore-based job. There were three deck-hands, Pam Desoutter, Mary Benwell and Tim Edridge, and Maureen, Margaret and I were to be *Anndora*'s stokers.

It turned out that *Anndora II* was the most elegant boat that we had ever handled. She had a graceful flared bow, with a spacious cabin amidships, and twin petrol engines on either side of her stern which gave her a cruising speed of fifteen knots. She had been bought from the RAF for the exclusive use of the Commander of Force Pluto, to convey him in style from one branch to another of his many-sided organization.

As we sped out of the Hamble and turned up Southampton Water, *Anndora*'s engines purred like a pedigree cat and clouds. of rainbow-tinted spray broke ecstatically over the bows. Fred began to sing 'Maggie May' at the top of his voice and we all wore ridiculous grins on our faces; it seemed as if we were to be the chosen few in a situation of exquisite enchantment.

The following day was my eighteenth birthday, and I celebrated it in a fitting manner. Maureen and Margaret each gave me fine illustrated books about famous seamen and mountaineers, and I received a number of parcels from home containing warm jerseys, socks and mufflers, and a white silk scarf for best. On the morning of the 17th I dressed myself in as many of my birthday presents as I could decently wear without arousing comment from higher authority, and we set off on the floating-bridge to Woolston, carrying a large square box which my mother had somehow contrived to have delivered to me a few minutes before our departure for work.

The morning was spent in learning semaphore on the quayside of *Abatos*, and after lunch we were initiated into the mysteries of knots and splices in the bosun's store. I shall always remember the pleasant hours we spent in that haven of warmth and shelter, far more hours than any of us suspected on that first day. There was a primitive iron stove with a long tapering chimney leading up through the roof of the shed. Fed with a plentiful supply of drift-wood from the Itchen, it crackled and sang happily whilst a warm glow soon pervaded the whole shed and augmented the irresistible smell of tarred rope, paraffin, oakum and other delicious substances which all add to the flavour of a bosun's store.

Fred Clarke sat on a large coil of manilla nearest to the stove, as befitted his rank, and we formed a semi-circle round him and marvelled at the adept way in which his fingers moved, in conjunction with a marline-spike, to form the most complicated rope designs called 'Turk's Heads' and 'Monkey's Fists', which all, apparently, had their uses in the scheme of nautical matters surrounding us.

Our working day ended soon after 4 pm, and 'Tea-boat' was announced. Fred produced a large tot of 'Neaters', the unadulterated rum served to naval ratings each day, and he divided it amongst us, giving me 'Double Sippers' as it was my birthday. We opened the square box and inside was a magnificent birthday cake with eighteen pink candles set in a sea of white icing, with a small silver anchor embedded below the legend 'Happy Birthday', which was picked out in pink icing. The anchor came from the TSS *Voltaire*, the old banana-ship on which we had travelled to West Africa in 1937. One of Fred's pals had gone down in her in 1941, when she was an armed merchant cruiser and had been sunk by a German ship in mid Atlantic. It was a solemn moment as we cut the cake in front of the stove in the bosun's store, and toasted the survivors of the TSS *Voltaire* in rum.

After such a promising introduction to HMS *Abatos*, things began to go wrong. We made one more voyage in *Anndora II* before she developed some serious engine trouble. I do not believe that we were responsible for this as even Margaret, who was always considered our star stoker, had not yet advanced beyond the simple daily maintenance stage, when faced with such a complicated piece of mechanism. But suddenly the engines refused, utterly and irrevocably, to start. A selection of engineering Petty Officers were sent for and rowed out to *Anndora II* by one of the deck-hands. Next day they returned with a Chief Petty Officer whose uniform fairly bristled with stars and propellers.

In the meantime the Commander of HMS *Abatos* strode up and down the quayside behaving like a rampageous bull and giving orders for that useless bevy of Wrens to be removed from his sight and put to work in any perishing place that could be found for them.

We were each given a copy of Nicholls's Seamanship and Nautical Knowledge which announced that it was intended. for Second Mates', Mates' and Masters' Examinations, and which told one just about everything, from how to tie a reef knot to the correct stowage of a cargo of Esparto Grass on a 3,000-ton freighter. With the help of this weighty tome and the nautical influence of our coxswain, we learnt a number of strange and wonderful things whilst seated on coils of hemp and manilla around the stove in the bosun's store.

It was not long before we realized that Fred had suffered many terrible experiences in the Arctic Convoys, and he was prone to deep fits of depression from time to time. I think Margaret was the only person who really understood him, and could help to bring him back from the horrors of total war to the kind of dream world in which we lived. None of us had been deeply hit by the war at this stage; we had not been bombed out of our homes, or lost our nearest and dearest, or been wounded or tortured by the Gestapo. We had no personal knowledge of the indescribable tragedies suffered by many people during a war, and some of us were inclined to regard the whole experience with the thoughtless egoism of extreme youth. Of all *Anndora*'s crew, perhaps Maureen was the most anxious for the war to finish, so that she could marry her Eric and go with him to live in Australia; but none of us had any means of fully understanding the state of mind to which Fred was sometimes reduced.

Day after day passed and *Anndora's* engines refused to show the faintest glimmer of life. We scrubbed and repainted the dinghies belonging to the base, studied Morse and semaphore until we became proficient signallers, learnt how to tie all sorts of knots, to splice rope and wire and to make rope fenders; then we began to study pilotage, buoyage and the Rule of the Road at Sea. It was a frustrating period in many ways as all of us longed to be at sea, doing some useful job on a boat.

One afternoon when we were off duty, Maureen and I took a bus to Portsmouth and went to visit Anne Norris who had been sent to HMS *Excellent*, the most sought after base in the Portsmouth Command. Poor Anne had a tale of woe to tell, which was incomparably greater than ours. It seemed that she had to work nearly all night, as well as during the day, and had not been issued with any warm waterproof clothing so that she was often soaked to the skin and freezing cold. We would gladly have changed places with her, but that was not to be.

On December 11th a miracle occurred; *Anndora II* was pronounced fit for work by the vast assembly of engineering experts who had tinkered with her engines during the past three weeks.

We set off along the River Itchen clad in our duffel-coats and sea-boots, as it had begun to snow that morning and there was a bitter east wind blowing across the river.

Once out in Southampton Water, Fred opened up the throttle and we sped towards Netley at 18 knots. Driving snow-flakes and hailstones mingled with the grey wintry sea-scape, and we were stunned by the icy blasts of air whenever we emerged from the wheel-house. Suddenly a thunderstorm exploded in the cold white heavens; there was a dull roar of thunder followed by a blinding flash of forked lightning, and a barrage-balloon caught fire. In a matter of seconds the fine silver skin had shrivelled into a flaming golden ball, and it landed in the water about twenty yards away from us with a sad prolonged sigh. Instinctively we pulled the hoods of our duffel-coats closer round our faces and peered at the smouldering water apprehensively, wearing the expressions of startled rabbits.

During that memorable outing we called alongside the Lilac and the Bustler to deliver signals to their Masters. At last *Anndora II* was proving her worth, and it was a cold but optimistic crew who moored their vessel out in mid Itchen that evening.

The following day we were due to take the Commander of HMS *Abatos* to Ryde. Early that morning we had been hard at work with our mops, scrubbers, Brasso and polishing rags, and by 10.30 am *Anndora* was fit to receive the King, we felt.

The Commander came aboard and ordered the engines to be started up. We tickled the carburettors and pressed the self-starters; nothing happened. We primed the cylinder heads and Margaret carefully examined the ignition system and cleaned round inside the distributor heads; still nothing happened. The Commander was pacing irritably up and down the deck, gnawing at his finger-nails. Suddenly our coxswain had an inspiration; he told us to remove all the sparking-plugs and he touched up their points with a lead pencil. We carefully replaced them, pressed the self-starters and the engines burst into life; two seconds later one of them burst into flames!

The Commander grabbed the Pyrene fire-extinguisher and squirted energetically. A miniature volcano of evil-smelling black smoke erupted from the engine, but the fire had been nipped in the bud, and so had the engine; a few seconds later the other engine petered out in sympathy with its twin.

Three times this performance took place, before we had both engines running smoothly and complacently. I recalled Chiefie's words about treating your engines like human beings rather than cold bits of metal, but I felt that this pair were definitely resistant to the milk of human kindness.

The Commander had no time or inclination to discuss the engines with sentiment. He engaged the clutch, opened the throttle wide, and almost before the deck-hands had had time to release the mooring-ropes we were roaring down the River Itchen, passing every other vessel in sight.

Out in Southampton Water the ever-increasing rows of tank landing-craft lurched uneasily at their moorings as we sped by in a great cloud of icy foam. The Commander was intent on reaching Ryde without any further delay.

Off Netley there was an ominous gurgling noise under the after deck-boards. I bent down and gingerly levered up one of them with a screwdriver, and a startling sight confronted me. *Anndora* had developed a serious leak round the stern-glands and water was gushing into the cockpit with the force of a soda-water syphon being manipulated by a thirsty man. Maureen sprang to the pump, but it was one of the old-fashioned variety which spent its time barking your knuckles, getting clogged with lumps of cotton-waste which had mysteriously found their way into the bilges and stubbornly refusing to cope with the ever-rising flood.

The Commander's eyebrows descended into a straight dark line, like a horizon before the storm breaks; and a thunderous explosive atmosphere overwhelmed the whole boat. He swung the wheel round and pointed *Anndora* back the way she had come, and the engines made such a deafening roar that we were unable to catch the terse phrases which escaped from his lips.

On arrival at HMS *Abatos* we all abandoned ship in two large friendly dinghies. *Anndora* began to settle into the dark oily embrace of the River Itchen, and when we came on duty the following morning, only her bows were visible above the swirling tide. Other ships came and went about their daily business, oblivious to the tragic fate of *Anndora II*.

The snow began to fall again, and, instinctively, we knew that our days at HMS *Abatos* were numbered.

HMS *ABATOS*

January 1944

Anndora II (my first boat), alongside some barges in the middle of the River Itchen.

Anndora and one of the diesel launches astern of her, at Abatos.

HMS *TORMENTOR*

July 1944

Winkle and I scrubbing out the stern of the
Camel alongside the Royal Pier.

The Camel starting off on a trip with Sue in the bows.

Boatscrew Wrens at Tormentor.

Left to Right:

Back Row: 'Pongo' de Castro, Catherine Macnab, Joyce Purll, Maureen Wells, Ann Galbraith, Freda Shemming, Pat Light, Pam Watson, Margaret Burton, Betty Price, Lone Grene.

Front Row: Joy Harper, Cynthia Gudgeon, 3/O Holloway, Mr. Anderson, Hugh Evans, Vera Richardson, Anne Woodruffe.

4

Rural Interludes

WE FILLED IN time until Christmas, manning a large Diesel launch whilst her crew were away on leave. It was a brief, but entirely satisfactory period. There was no engine trouble and all day long we ran out to the Force Pluto ships in Southampton Water, delivering stores and signals and bringing men ashore. The combination of hard work and cold sea air suited us all ideally, and for a few days we were supremely happy.

All too soon it was Christmas Day. The night before, the six of us who shared a cabin had hung up our sea-boot socks hopefully at the end of our bunks. In the middle of the night, when everyone judged that all the others would be asleep, there was a short period of sheer chaos; six hefty Boats' Crew Wrens were all stumbling around in the dark at the same time, filling each other's stockings, falling over furniture, treading on cockroaches with bare feet and swearing strange oaths in the black night.

On Christmas Day we had a great banquet served by the Wren Officers. I felt rather homesick and not up to sharing the gleeful anticipation with which some of the girls at HMS *Shrapnel* looked forward to receiving their grub from the hands of their superiors. I think this entertainment appealed to the officers' stewards most of all, but there was a false air of joviality about the whole thing, for Christmas, after all, is a family concern.

In the evening we went to a dance at the Seamen's Mission and, having grown bolder since our preliminary ventures in Portsmouth, I took up a conspicuous position near the door and fixed one or two likely looking men with my eye. Much to my surprise, in a matter of a few seconds I was swept on to the floor by an immensely tall and silent sailor. He revealed that his name was Lofty, but beyond this fact I gleaned no further information from him. He navigated amongst the jitterbugging Americans with enormous skill and composure, and some of the other girls from *Shrapnel* cast envious glances in our direction.

Boxing Day was remarkable for two things; a notable lack of enthusiasm for work exhibited by most of us; and the sinking of the German battleship *Scharnhorst*.

On New Year's Eve I went home for ten days' leave. It was an unexpectedly difficult period. Instead of luxuriating in the comfort and security of my home, I found that I missed the life in Southampton bitterly and was most ungrateful for all the parties which my mother had been at some pains to arrange for me.

There was a battalion of the Scot's Guards stationed in and around our home at that time, and I met a number of the officers and their wives at a thé dansant which took place on New Year's Day. I was fairly red in outlook after two and a half years at Mansfield Grammar School and a few months as a rating in the WRNS, and this party was a most alarming social experience. A handful of charming and suitable young men had been selected as partners for me, but our conversation seemed, invariably, to progress along different wave-lengths. The following dialogue was fairly typical...

SP (Suitable Partner)—'Would you care to dance?'

Me—'Thank you, I should love to.' (We move on to the dance floor, I trip over his right foot and tread heavily down on his toes, forget Maureen's advice until it is too late and apologize profusely.)

SP—'Are you going to the Cholmondeley-Davenport's ball next week?'

Me—'No, I've never heard of them, and anyway I shall be back at work again by then.'

SP (peering at my oil-engrained fingers with repulsion)—'Work! Whatever sort of work do you find to do?'

Me (standing on tiptoe to achieve an extra inch above my normal height)—'I am a stoker in the WRNS.'

SP (unimpressed)—'What a comic idea! Boats always make me vomit. What a relief it must be to come home on leave?'

Me—'Well, not exactly you see I love working on a boat and the people down there are smashing.'

SP—'Smashing? Is that a new word used by the hoi polloi?'

At that moment an elegant brunette, the wife of a rather agreeable Captain in the same regiment, glided across the floor and, pinching the right ear-lobe of my partner, whispered 'Darling!' in a husky conspiratorial manner. The music stopped and I escaped to sit in the lavatory for half an hour, in case some other SPs should be found for me to dance with.

Later that evening there was an electric power cut which lasted for twenty minutes or so. The whole party was plunged into darkness and my father sent me to grope for candles and matches in his desk on the far side of the room. I found what I was looking for, but suddenly became aware of a faint scuffling noise near my left foot; I lit a match and there was the brunette bitch in the arms of SP, beneath the desk! It was a trivial incident and I did not tell my parents about it afterwards. But I had, at that age, already begun to develop idealistic views on marriage, and somehow I felt outraged and let down that my father's desk had been used to shelter such a couple.

On the tenth morning I conned my uniform with pride once more, and travelled back to that other world which I had grown to love. Joyful strains of the 'Blue Danube' pursued the Southampton train out of Waterloo Station, and a sailor who had secured a seat with his mate in the compartment behind me, exclaimed—'Cor! Stone the crows! If that ain't a female stoker, Bill! What's the perishin' navy comin' to? Move up and give 'er a pew.'

There had been a long and complicated inquiry into the sinking of *Anndora II* during our absence. First the blame was attached to Fred Clarke because he had done nothing to quench the leak before we abandoned ship. But the Commander had roared at him to let the flaming boat sink and hurry up and get into the flaming dinghy; and as six of us had been there as witnesses, this line of inquiry was soon abandoned. Then the blame was fastened in turn on to the Chief Petty Officer who had passed the boat as fit on the previous day, and the boatyard for handing her over in such a condition; but they responded by announcing that the Commander was entirely to blame because of the way in which he had handled *Anndora*. Thus the blame was batted backwards and forwards like a ping-pong ball, until it was finally attached to the RAF in a vague sort of way, for selling us the boat in the first place.

None of this business helped us towards finding a boat to work on again. *Anndora* was fished up from the bed of the Itchen and returned to the boatyard for further investigations. In the meantime we spent our days baling half-frozen water out of the dinghies, rowing officers to and from ships in mid-river, signalling frantically to keep our circulation going and making rope fenders in the bosun's store.

Maureen's leave had been extended for several weeks as she fell ill whilst at home, and Margaret had a bad cold and cough which hung on through the bleak days of January. We had all of us reached our lowest ebb when a stroke of good fortune smote us with the swiftness of an arrow. On January 27th, Maureen, Margaret and I were sent on draft to HMS *Tormentor* at Warsash, to get some practical experience on boats until we should be needed at *Abatos* again.

In January, 1944, HMS *Tormentor* was a real Combined Ops. working base and no nonsense about it. The River Hamble was filled with rows, known as trots, of Tank Landing Craft, Infantry Landing Craft and Assault Landing Craft, right from the mouth up to the bridge at Bursledon.

The Wrens were housed in attractive villas with names like 'Sunburst', 'Tideways' and 'Hamblemeads', strung out along the saddle of a line of hills commanding a fine view over the Solent and the mouth of the River Hamble. The headquarters of the base was an imposing red brick building which is now the Household Brigade Yacht Club.

There were sixteen Boats' Crew Wrens at *Tormentor*, divided into two watches, each working from 8 am till midday one day, and from midday until nearly midnight the next. They came under the immediate jurisdiction of a Warrant Officer known as the Bosun. There were five boats at their disposal, the *Crash-Boat*, *Dove*, *Sea-Gull*, *Sea-Rat*, and

Sea-Mouse, and they were kept running day and night, whatever the weather conditions. These boats did all the fetching and carrying for the landing-craft attached to the base; amongst their varied cargoes, mixed haphazardly together, were senior officers, urgent signals, hospital cases, sacks of potatoes, barrels of rum and drunken sailors returning to their ships in the last liberty-boats.

The wheat was soon sifted from the chaff amongst the Boats' Crew Wrens at *Tormentor*, for the work was tough and arduous during the cold days of winter, and those who had joined with an eye to the glamour of idling on a boat during the halcyon days of summer were quickly disillusioned. They usually changed to other categories or the married ones became pregnant so that they could get themselves discharged from the Wrens.

Amongst those who stood the pace there was a Petty Officer Coxswain called Jimmy Edwards, who had a Yacht Master's Ticket and had been in command of various famous yachts before the war. She was the only person who dared show a total disregard for the many rules and regulations constantly being instituted by the Wren Officers at the base. When round hats were introduced for Wrens, Jimmy continued to wear the old-fashioned squashed-lemon-shaped variety; when an order was re-enforced, absolutely forbidding the possession of any four-legged pets at the base, Jimmy continued to flaunt a small off-white doormat of a bitch, known as Sue-Dog, which slept on the end of her bunk in the Wrens' quarters and invariably accompanied her to sea when she was on duty.

Jimmy Edwards was a hard taskmaster, as she loved the sea and boats more than anything else in the world and she was the complete perfectionist in all her nautical manoeuvres, and expected her crew to rise to the same Olympian heights. Time meant nothing to Jimmy, and there was no question of knocking off duty at an appointed hour. If there was any work outstanding on one of the boats, and she usually contrived to find some, one might spend the entire evening upside-down in the bilges poking at some obscure apertures with a marline-spike in order to induce the bilge water to flow freely. Meanwhile one's friends would be enjoying themselves at a dance or an ENSA concert in the base. But it was not until much later that I became Jimmy's crew.

On our first arrival at HMS *Tormentor*, Margaret and I worked together on the *Dove*, a small launch with twin Thornycroft engines which was used for transporting officers and signals. Our coxswain was a cheerful robust girl called Cynthia Gudgeon, who ignored all our fumbling inexperience and laughed her way out of any delicate situations caused by her new crew.

We went on duty at 8 am on our third morning at Warsash. Margaret was acting as deck-hand that day, whilst I took charge of the engines. It was still dark as we prepared the *Dove* for her first trip; I lifted up a five-gallon drum of lubricating oil, thinking it was petrol, and poured the entire contents into the petrol tanks. The results were disastrous; at midday, when we came off duty, the *Dove* was definitely out of action.

Soon after this highly embarrassing occurrence Margaret and I were transferred to the *Sea-Rat*, a large open cutter with a Kelvin engine which, no doubt, was considered tough enough to withstand my daily maintenance and running repairs. We used to take turns at being stoker or deck-hand, the latter job being much favoured except in the coldest weather when a certain amount of warmth could be derived from the proximity of the engine.

The deck-hand always stood in the bows of the boat whilst under way, acting as a look-out and holding on to the sides of ships with a long boat-hook whilst men and stores were being transhipped. It was a position of a certain enviability, for one was at a higher elevation than either the coxswain or stoker, and could, therefore, see much more of what was going on in the boat. On the last run at night, when all the liberty men were returning to their ships, it was the deck-hand's job to see that no man was lost overboard. Sometimes there were as many as seventy men aboard, many of them drunk, and it took a strong and experienced deck-hand, on occasion, to deliver all those men safely back to the right ships!

Despite these hazards, there was something irresistibly lovely about the night runs at *Tormentor*. I remember one night early in February, when a hard frost had settled on the decks and the air was breathtakingly cold. Above us hung a dark velvet canopy illuminated by a crescent moon, a million stars and a pattern of criss-cross ladders of light, all the searchlights in Southampton probing the northern sky for a lone German raider. I stood in the bows, holding a boat-hook in one hand like a crusader's banner and an Aldis lamp in the other, which I shone on all the ships, buoys and jetties for Cynthia to see. As the powerful light danced amongst the forest of masts and derricks, I contemplated the unutterable beauty of that shining river flowing quietly beneath the starry heavens. Behind me some men were singing 'Danny Boy', very softly as befitted such a night, and I knew then that I had reached the ultimate peak of happiness in all my eighteen years.

The days passed so quickly at Warsash that I lost all count of time. Life was a constant cycle of leaping out of bed on cold dark mornings, gulping a few mouthfuls of scalding-hot tea and bread and margarine, then cycling down the muddy country lanes in a semi-bemused condition until we reached the river; either *Tormentor* Pier or the Rising Sun Pier would be our destination, where our sleeping boats were moored. There never seemed enough time to refuel the boat, examine the oil dipstick and re-stuff all the grease caps before Cynthia was shouting at us to cast off for'ard and aft and look sharp about it.

The first trip was usually a run up the Hamble to Bursledon, picking up stores parties from the infantry landing-craft all the way. Sometimes the flotillas were out at sea and we would have time to watch the pale wintry sun piercing the early morning mist, which clung tenaciously to the drowsy river. Then Margaret and I would fill our buckets with hot water from the exhaust pipe and start to scrub the *Sea-Rat*. That ritual of scrubbing out was a daily occurrence which we undertook with pride and enjoyment, despite the shock of plunging our icy hands into boiling water which caused them to resemble under-done cuts of prime sirloin when seen amongst the softer whiter hands of our friends at home.

When business was slack on the river, Cynthia would sometimes bring the *Sea-Rat* alongside a beautiful old steam yacht called the

Melisande, moored off Hamble. She had been taken over by the navy for the duration, and the Petty Officer in charge would usually contrive to have three huge mugs of tea, laced with rum, waiting for us whenever we hove in sight.

When the flotillas came in from the sea, there was always a great deal of work to do. If a strong wind was blowing up the river, we had to come alongside them whilst they were still under way and take a mooring-line from their bows to the nearest buoy up-wind. This was a job which called for perfect judgement and synchronization of manoeuvres on the part of both coxswains, and sometimes it ended in a chaotic entanglement of vessels and ropes and a sharp interchange of fruity abuse between the two craft.

One morning we had had a particularly trying time mooring half a dozen ships in a driving snow-storm, with the wind at right angles to the tide. They had entered the river just before midday, causing us to be very late in coming off duty. Margaret was stoking that day, whilst I acted as deck-hand; and all three of us were feeling exceedingly cold and surly, as we had certainly missed our lunch at Hamblemeads. As we approached the Rising Sun Pier after this ordeal, I noticed a Petty-Officer, a man whose physiognomy reminded me of a wild boar I had once seen at close quarters in the Ardennes, leaning over the railing at the end of the pier. The *Sea-Mouse* was already moored there, so we came alongside her and I climbed across to secure our bow-line to one of her for'ard cleats. My hands were so cold that I had difficulty in pulling on the wet rope, let alone making it fast.

'You there!' roared a harsh grating voice above me. 'Is that a boat you're tying up, or an effing Christmas parcel? Time you learnt a few simple bends and hitches.'

I kept my head down and pretended I hadn't heard, but all the time my numbed fingers were moving with lightning speed, trying to prove what an excellent job I could make of securing the boat.

On alternate days we were on duty from midday until nearly midnight. The afternoon trips always seemed more relaxed; most of the stores parties were back aboard their ships by then, and we usually brought liberty men ashore on the first three trips after lunch, then started taking them back again after 8 pm.

That narrow winding river, the haunt of countless yachtsmen in times of peace, had become the supreme focus of our existence during the bleak winter days of 1944. It flowed endlessly up and down, the flood and the ebb tides moving by in tones of grey and sepia, with a rhythmic certainty which whispered of eternity. All the way up the river we had established a line of friendly ships, known as 'tea and chocolate ships', floating havens where we were assured of finding a cup of warm liquid awaiting us on an icy winter's night. How good they tasted, those scalding mugs which we clasped in our hands whilst standing on the frozen decks of an infantry landing-craft, our breath forming strange patterns as it spiralled upwards through the still cold air.

During most of those magic days poor Maureen was away on compassionate leave, looking after her mother who was dangerously ill, and it was not until we had been at Warsash for over two weeks that she rejoined us.

On our afternoons off duty Margaret and I were usually too tired to do more than sit in front of a big fire in the Wrens' quarters, reading, darning and writing letters. However, on February 14th, the same day that Maureen returned, we were invited to a Valentine's Dance at Hamble. We scrubbed our lanyards, polished our shoes and put on clean white shirts, collars and black ties, garments which we seldom wore at other times.

The eight o'clock liberty-boat from the Rising Sun Pier was filled with Wrens and sailors from *Tormentor* going to the dance. How strange it seemed to be sitting on a thwart in the middle of the boat, dressed in our Sunday best, with no engine to mind or Aldis lamp to shine on the dark objects we were passing. I ran my fingers along the thwart to see if it had been properly scrubbed that day, and watched the duty crew at work with a critical eye.

Melodious strains of dance music wafted out across the black water as we drew near to Hamble Pier. Margaret and I had already begun to worry about our tactics on arrival at the dance, but our fears of being wall-flowers were soon dispelled. The little dance-hall was overflowing with naval uniforms and we had hardly squeezed through the door before half a dozen familiar voices called out greetings:

'Whatcher, Stokes! Thought they'd locked you up after the way you 'andled that gear-box last night! Make room for Curly, Sunshine and Little Maggie, boys! Whatcher wan' te drink? Pint o' black an' tan? Doncher listen te 'im, Blondie. Come an' do a foxtrot wiv me.'

From that moment onwards we never sat down. The band played old-time waltzes, quicksteps, foxtrots, Lambeth Walks, Palais Glides, rhumbas, sambas and congas; and we danced and danced and the men sang their hearts out until it seemed that the roof must rise off the building and float away skywards until it touched the stars.

That evening I became aware of a new sensation which I had never met before; the feeling of belonging to one great family, all working together towards some glorious end. It was a warm protective feeling which exists on many ships I believe, but seldom in the larger sterner world outside.

Two days later we had only been on duty for a couple of hours before the three of us were sent for by the First Officer at the base and told that we had been recalled to HMS *Abatos*, and must, therefore, pack and return to Southampton immediately. It was a bitter blow, and three very forlorn and unhappy Wren Stokers climbed aboard the bus to Southampton later that afternoon.

Jimmie driving No 1 (the original LCPL) with Sue-dog on deck.

Jimmie and Sue-dog in *Alanna* alongside
the jetty in the Engineering Yard.

September 1944

Penny coxing the *Camel* with Su Taylor and Jean scrubbing out.

The *Camel* at the Yankee fuelling jetty. Penny,
Jean, Su and one of the Yanks in the boat.

Su Taylor coxing the *Camel*.

Looking up for'ard on the 8 am trip—off Netley.

5

Poseidon amongst the Primroses

THE LAST TWO weeks of February dragged by in a slow and mournful manner. All around us things were happening, enormously exciting things which might change the whole course of history, but we were mere onlookers, unable to take part in this magnificent gesture against the years of oppression in occupied Europe.

Each day there were new and wonderful flat-bottomed vessels of every size, shape and description, moored out on the trots in Southampton Water. Big chunks of 'Mulberries', the prefabricated harbours which were to play such an important part in the landing of equipment on the coast of Normandy, grew overnight like enchanted mushrooms. One day there was a miniature breakwater moored out in midstream on the River Test, and the next day it had grown into some vast amphibious harbour wall, an ingenious challenge to the wrath of Poseidon.

Then the Americans began to arrive in their LSTs (Landing Ship-Tanks), immense unwieldy vessels camouflaged in sombre tones of khaki and urine-green to match the English Channel in wintertime. They disgorged several thousand soldiers and sailors on to British soil and the fertile spirit of animosity flourished. The Yanks were better paid and clothed, and they often received sumptuous parcels of food and nylon stockings from home, so many of the girls preferred their company. The British sailors did not care for these boastful gum-chewing allies, and they gave us due warning of their sentiments.

'If ever we see one of you girls out with a Yank or a bit o' gold braid, we won't never speak te you again, see,' a signalman on the *Lilac* promised us; and those who ignored his advice found that it was no idle threat, but something which the English seamen felt very strongly about.

Nearly every night there were fights between the Yanks and the British servicemen. Often knives were drawn and the ambulances were kept busy rushing casualties to hospital.

The days passed, and we filled in time at *Abatos* as best we could. *Anndora II* was back on her mooring again, apparently no worse for her misadventures the previous month. But at last the idea had occurred to higher authority that we were too large a crew for such a small vessel, so the honour of manning her was strictly rationed; this meant that each of us was lucky if we achieved as many as two trips a week. The rest of the time on duty was spent in baling icy water out of *Anndora's* bilges for she seemed to leak just as much whether she was running or stationary—endlessly polishing the brasswork, doing occasional short trips in another boat called *Skylark II*, and scrubbing out some new Wren quarters in a house in Archer's Road.

Pay Day was once a fortnight. We stokers earned £1 12s 6d, and on receipt of this handsome sum we would take it in turns to treat the others to milk shakes and jam tarts at the Tudor Café.

If our days on duty seemed uninspired, our free time was less so. Margaret and I frequently went to the cinema and to concerts at the NAAFI, or to dances at the Guildhall where I was sometimes lucky enough to find Lofty, towering emphatically above his fellow men. We danced together a great deal but I did not discover where he came from, what his real name was or anything much about him. Perhaps it was better that way; the enjoyment of dancing without any of the interchange of background information and involvement which usually ensued. Anyway we continued to waltz and foxtrot around the crowded dance-halls of Southampton, and all my carefully laid traps for ensnaring him into some intimate revelations were about as effective as a mosquito trying to draw blood from Nelson's Column.

Whenever there was enough time I cycled over to Hamble and caught the next liberty-boat down-river to Warsash. Those days were filled with rather nostalgic encounters, and I usually returned to Southampton feeling intensely sorry for myself.

At the beginning of March my mother came south to spend a week-end at Lyndhurst in the New Forest. I had obtained a sleeping-out pass for the Saturday night, and there was a cheerful holiday feeling in the air as I caught the bus to Lyndhurst that morning. We lunched in great style at the Crown Hotel, then we went for a walk in the forest. All the trees were throwing off their winter mantles and sprouting fat green buds which seemed about to burst into song like young sopranos; and there were hundreds and thousands of primroses growing in large friendly clumps amidst the rich green moss and the tangled undergrowth of the forest. I heard a blackbird warbling in an oak tree, and suddenly the war seemed very far away. How could one rationalize a world which contained bombers and blackbirds, barrage-balloons and beech buds, periscopes and primroses, all in the same breath?

We continued our walk through the New Forest as far as Minstead where we stopped for tea at the Honeysuckle Cottage, a noble repast which included hot buttered scones and home-made raspberry jam. At some point during that meal, when my mouth was full of the local specialities, my mother began to question me minutely, as all mothers are apt to do, about my evenings off duty; what sort of parties I went to, who I met there and whether there were any suitable young men in the offing. Masticating a hot scone at top speed, my answer was a masterpiece of evasion and lightning invention, for I could not imagine her viewing the Valentine's dance at Hamble with much favour, nor yet the hops which we attended at the Seamen's Mission and the Guildhall, or the singsongs in the NAAFI Club.

There was a heavy snowfall during the night, no doubt sent to discourage the first heady murmurings of springtime. On Sunday morning we went to church in the village of Lyndhurst, then Margaret came over by bus to join us and that afternoon we strolled across a shimmering white carpet pierced, here and there, by the fragile yellow heads of primroses. The idyllic week-end was soon over; my mother left for the north, whilst Margaret and I returned to Southampton and the excitement of preparations for the Second Front.

During the following week it seemed that matters were conspiring towards an improvement in our working days. Fred received orders to teach us boat-hook drill, both stokers and deck-hands alike, and we took *Anndora* out for one or two short runs, to Hamble to refuel and to various ships moored near the, mouth of the River Itchen.

On March 7th the Commander and a Wren Officer with a Pekinese dog came aboard, and we ran down Southampton Water and westwards along the Solent to Lepe, where *Anndora* went alongside the *Persephone* and the *Glenmoriston* whilst the Commander called on their skippers. I was bow-man that day, and I felt rather foolish performing gymnastic feats with the boat-hook alongside a rust-streaked tub like the old YO-YO Ship, with the Pekinese, which had climbed on to the for'ard deck, snapping round my ankles. I took a surreptitious swipe at it when the Wren Officer was looking the other way, and one of the seamen leant over the deck-rail and whispered: 'Garn, Stokes! Kick it up the arse before she turns round!' A moment later the Commander appeared on deck with *Persephone's* skipper: he found me standing to attention with the boat-hook held at the ready to bear off for'ard, my face a mask of pure maidenly innocence.

That voyage to Lepe was the highlight of our sea-going experiences with Force Pluto. The only other remarkable events during that week were the Wren Superintendent's visit to HMS *Abatos*, and the bursting into flames of one of *Anndora's* engines, which had a reminiscent flavour about it.

Things seemed to be going downhill again. We continued our daily sessions of baling icy bilge water out of *Anndora*, as, for some obscure reason, the pump never seemed to work. And to add to our discomfort, a great storm arose in sea area Wight and the River Itchen was transformed into a swirling seething grey cauldron, in the middle of which we succeeded in getting the stern mooring-rope caught securely round *Anndora's* port propeller. A sultry and unpleasant atmosphere resulted from this manoeuvre; luckily Margaret and I were off duty next day and we took a train to Bournemouth to forget about our troubles. After a few hours spent in shop gazing and playing with the slot-machines on the end of the pier, *Anndora*'s mishaps seemed to diminish in importance and I found myself longing for the life aboard a proper working boat instead of this capricious officer's toy.

Next day Maureen and I were sent on draft back to HMS *Tormentor*. It was the answer to our prayers and we were both delighted at this unexpected turn in our fortunes, but for one thing; we felt very sad at leaving Margaret behind. She, for her part, although she was sorry to see us go, was, I believe, secretly glad to be staying at *Abatos*. She had been chosen as the best stoker to look after *Anndora*'s engines, she felt a sort of maternal pride and fondness for Force Pluto and all who served in it, and Fred Clarke, our coxswain, would have been lost without little Maggie to keep him from brooding on his past.

Maureen and I arrived back at Warsash on March 15th and were sent to live in a small house called Hookbye, about a mile away from *Tormentor* Pier. Maureen found herself sharing a cabin with Patricia Mountbatten, who was a Wren Plotter at *Tormentor* at that time. She was a quiet girl, with none of the social inclinations which were expected of her, and she knew exactly how to deal with ambitious young officers who tried to date her with an eye to their future careers.

The day after our arrival I went to work on the *Sea-Gull*, with Sheila Norbury as my coxswain. There were only two of us to run the boat so that we shared all the engine maintenance and daily scrubbing between us, and whilst we were under way Sheila steered and worked the engine controls whilst I acted as bow-man. It was an ideal arrangement as far as I was concerned, and the warmth of the sun during those mid-March days helped to make our job one which I would not have exchanged for the life of a millionaire.

The first days of spring came and went in a joyful cycle. We watched the sun rise over the headquarters of HMS *Tormentor* on our early morning trips. All day long the *Sea-Gull* ran up and down the Hamble, carrying men, stores and signals to the ever-increasing rows of landing-craft; then we saw the sun set like a ball of burnished copper behind the Fairey Aviation Works, and the stars come out, one by one, until the whole vast sky was alight with a million diamond pellets, and the searchlights of Portsmouth and Southampton vied for brilliance with Sirius and Orion's Belt.

The routine was always the same; but there were changes taking place around us all the time. Near to Hookbye there was a small wood of silver birch trees and already they were clothed with a fine tracery of tender green leaves, whilst beneath them lurked some fat glistening clumps of primroses. Amongst the taller trees the birds were singing their hearts out, and down by the river young seagulls with soft brown feathers and unsteady wings were listening to the deep contemplative chuckles of their proud parents. Scarcely a buoy, beacon or mooring-post was vacant on such delightful spring mornings.

The river and the sky; they seemed to fill our lives in those days, and they were changing too. Each morning there was a deeper and more vivid shade of blue amongst the round white cumulus clouds, and the sombre grey river began to reflect these splendid colours until there were pools of cabochon sapphires and emeralds spreading outwards in ever-widening circles.

On days when business was slack and the Bosun was out of sight, I used to lie across the bows of the *Sea-Gull* watching the rainbow in our bow-wave as we navigated across the dancing waters. I had never known that life could be so good before.

One afternoon when Maureen and I were both off duty, we cycled over to Southampton to visit Margaret at HMS *Abatos*. Nothing had changed there and I felt ridiculously thankful when I heard that we should never be sent back there again. At that moment my only wish in life was to remain at *Tormentor* until the end of the war.

Shortly after this outing poor Maureen started running a temperature and was put to bed in the sick-bay. I changed boats to the *Sea-Rat*, to take her place as crew under a coxswain called Anne Woodruff.

Working with Anne was a much more adventurous business than anything I had hitherto experienced. For one thing her parents lived on the Isle of Wight and she always contrived to get the *Sea-Rat* sent on any errands to the island. One of the first trips we did together was to take an officer back to his ship, moored off Cowes. We left *Tormentor* Pier at 6.30 am and ran at half speed through an impenetrable white fog. Anne steered by compass whilst I stood in the bows, keeping a good look-out for any buoys or ships across our course. Presently the rising sun began to probe the sea-fog with its long golden fingers; from time to time we saw a ship, a ghostly phantom vessel floating in an unsubstantial pool of iridescent vapours. I could hear fog-horns and bell-buoys, and the solemn swish of smooth grey water running past our hull; and then there were dozens of ships all around us, their anchor bells joining in the early morning chorus. We came alongside a sheer black hull, as tall as the cliffs of Dover, and our officer jumped on to a flimsy rope ladder and sped up into the clouds like a monkey in a date palm. As we passed under her stern I looked up at her name; *Maid of Orleans*... surely I had crossed to Boulogne in her once when I was a child.

The last days of March drifted by in a happy whirl of nautical activities, and the sun shone down upon us with unaccustomed warmth. There was one memorable morning which I shall never forget. We had done our usual early run up the Hamble, picking up stores parties from all the landing-craft and bringing them ashore. There was an hour to spare and Anne decided to take the *Sea-Rat* across to the Shellmex Pier to refuel. No sooner had we cast off than she handed me the tiller and went up for'ard to turn out a locker in the bows. It was the first time I had ever steered a boat and, without a moment's warning, the whole course of my future life was altered! The magnificent thrill and enchantment of holding that quivering piece of wood and controlling the fate of a restless vibrant boat! That glorious harmony of a man and his boat (or a woman and her boat), sharing the perils of the deep and exploring the unknown watery wastes of our planet... My mind raced ahead to a future of improbably dangerous exploits and unimagined maritime bliss... And suddenly there was a great jetty looming up ahead of me and I couldn't remember which way to push the tiller.

During my hours off duty I felt rather lonely with neither of my two special friends to go out with. Most days I used to visit Maureen in the sick-bay and sit there chattering for as long as the Sister would allow it. Maureen had some fascinating theories on the psychology of colours and how a careful selection and blending of certain hues, worn by different people, could affect the thoughts and tempers of those who had to share their lives. I had never heard this idea expounded before and often tried my hardest to disprove it, but Maureen always stuck to her guns with the tenacity of a limpet.

At other times I used to lie on the shingle beach below Sunburst, and watch the pageant of shipping steaming up and down the Solent and the clouds sailing up and down the pale blue heavens.

On April 1st there was a complete change in the weather. March had come in and gone out like a lamb that year, but the hungry raging lion was lurking just around the corner. With a suddenness which took us all by surprise, a deep depression swept in from the Atlantic and Poseidon let loose upon the English Channel all the elemental furies in his domain. For three or four days a mighty deluge of rain descended upon the earth, whilst the wind howled and shrieked in the rigging with a primeval violence which defied all the tender whisperings of springtime. Puny mortals cowered in their houses or cabins, but when they were forced to be abroad, negotiated their business with the utmost possible dispatch.

For us there was no respite from the gale. It had been ordained that the *Sea-Rat* should make a trip up and down the trots on the Hamble every two hours, and no one saw any necessity to modify this law. Always drenched to the skin and half blinded by the driving rain and spray, we manned our gallant vessel like the Vikings did in ancient times; the brims of our streaming sou'westers formed gullies through which the water funnelled with the force of a mountain stream upon any unfortunate person who approached within range.

On the first night of the gale we did not finish work until 2 am. When at last the boat was moored safely by the Rising Sun Pier, we groped our way ashore half dead with cold and lack of sleep, and there, to our delight, were two steaming mugs of chocolate and rum which the sentry on duty at the end of the pier had prepared for us in his little hut. Never had I tasted such an ambrosial beverage before!

That first week of April passed in a timeless routine of work and sleep of which our numbed limbs and senses were scarcely aware. By the end of the week the weather had begun to moderate and we threw off our saturated oilskins and peered optimistically at the small blue patches of sky amongst the heavy grey storm clouds. I stood on the bows and inhaled deeply of the fresh salt breeze blowing in from the west; at the same moment I noticed the Bosun, apparently awaiting our arrival, standing on the end of *Tormentor* Pier. A premonition of impending disaster gripped me as we secured the *Sea-Rat* alongside the pier.

'Well, Pierrepont, it looks as if we shall have to get along without your artistic sheepshanks and fisherman's bends,' he announced with a malicious grin spreading from one ear to the other. They want you back in Southampton again, so you'd better look sharp and get back to the base to see First Officer before you leave.'

I climbed up the iron ladder on to the pier, remembered that I hadn't said goodbye to Anne, went back down the ladder to mumble a few unintelligible words, then up again for the last time. I jumped on to my bicycle and pedalled fast along the muddy track which fringed the shore. Brambles and long branches with sharp talons tried to clutch me and impede my progress, but I pedalled blindly on, oblivious to all my surroundings.

Winkle coxing the *Camel* Off Town Quay.

Winkle coxing the *Camel* Bringing men
ashore from Hythe and E Trot.

The MN Mail Boat out in the Solent.

Left to Right: Half-Pint, Winkle, Taffy, Stox, and Sue.

Lt Sherwood ('Horrible Horace') standing
near the *Camel* at Parson's Hard.

6

HMS *Squid*

To BEGIN WITH there was nothing right about Southampton. I hated it all with a bitter unreasoning hatred; the streets, the docks, the big merchant ships, the Yanks, in fact all my fellow creatures. I had been sent alone, without either of my friends, to a horrid new base with an equally horrid name; HMS *Squid*... whoever thought of naming one of His Majesty's ships after such a repulsive cephalopod?

The Wrens' quarters were in a mock Tudor dwelling set amongst overgrown laurels in the totally unattractive suburb of Shirley. I arrived at Bridell Lodge, my new home, resembling a tired and dirty tramp; my suitcase overlapped the carrier on the back of my bicycle and various paper parcels were insecurely attached to the handlebars by odd bits of codline. There was no one about and the gloomy laurels regarded me with hostile stares, yet another intruder into their Victorian privacy.

I penetrated the house through a door at the rear and found a depressed-looking girl peeling potatoes in the galley. She surveyed my arrival without enthusiasm and supposed that I was one of the new Boats' Crew Wrens and, therefore, had better dump my belongings in the Boats' Crew cabin. I agreed with her supposition and followed her into a small, dark, intensely overcrowded room, into which ten bunks in double tiers had been wedged, along with five chests-of-drawers. Before abandoning me, the potato-peeling Wren informed me that this cabin was shared by twenty girls who worked in twenty-four hour watches, so that the bunks hardly ever had time to grow cold . . s. as soon as one lot vacated them, the others jumped in! And, furthermore, there was no point in unpacking as all the drawers and hanging space was already occupied.

She left the room and I sat down on one of the lower bunks and burst into tears. I cannot remember for how long I crouched there, indulging in an orgy of self-pity, before an odd impression began to penetrate my fuddled faculties. There was one corner of that hideous dismal cabin which had a vaguely familiar look about it; certain luxurious trappings arranged tastefully in the smallest conceivable space; a subtle air of comfort and homeliness about the whole thing, which pleased the eye. Suddenly the mystery was solved for the door opened to admit Anne Norris, the girl who had been on our stoker's course in Portsmouth. Seldom have I been more pleased than at that moment, to see an old friend walk into a room.

Anne took me under her wing and made it her business to cheer me up. Later that day we cycled down to the Royal Pier which runs out into the River Test opposite some extensive mud flats called the Gymp. The old band-room on the end of the pier had been turned over to the Boats' Crew Wrens as their living quarters whilst on duty. It was usually known as HMS *Gannet*; a gannet being a sailor's nickname for a greedy person!

The band-room was divided into two apartments; a long narrow room with immense windows along one side, where we slept in a row of double bunks if there was any time to sleep, and washed at the far end of it in a cluster of tin basins. And a half-moon-shaped room which was our mess and sitting-room, with a small galley adjoining. The floor of this room was covered with coconut matting, charts were pinned up around the walls, a long deal table extended down one side and an old charcoal stove stood in the curve of the half-moon. Around the stove were grouped two ancient brown leather armchairs and an odd assortment of upright chairs of varying degrees of discomfort.

There were fourteen Boats' Crew Wrens attached to HMS *Squid* at that period, and they had only two boats moored alongside the Royal Pier, neither of which was in working order. Six of those girls had been trained as stokers, and they had already been in Southampton for several months without ever setting foot on a boat. It was a depressing prospect, but before I had time to brood on it Anne started introducing me to some of the others and to the Wren who was in charge there that day. I took an instant dislike to her which I soon discovered was mutual. One of the laziest girls I ever met, her favourite occupation was to lounge in one of the armchairs with her feet up on the stove and discuss, in a loud and resonant voice, the more intimate details of her married life. She had quite a large following who liked nothing better than to be included in these conversations, and the last thing they seemed to want was to find themselves crewing on a boat which actually worked.

Later that afternoon Anne took me round to the boats' office at the end of Town Quay to meet Lt Horace Sherwood who was directly in charge of us during our working hours. He was a big man with brown hair, a craggy red face and delphinium blue eyes, partially concealed under ferocious overhanging eyebrows. His chin had a hard determined set to it and his whole appearance was at once striking and somewhat alarming.

The telephone rang in the boats' office and Lt Sherwood lifted the receiver:

'I heard you only too damn well!' he roared, after the briefest possible murmurings from the other end of the phone. 'And I don't want any interference with my Wrens from some old cow up at headquarters. They're here to do a job of work on the perishing boats and not to toady around in white collars saying "Yes, Ma'am; No, Ma'am; Three bags full, Ma'am". Have we got that point quite clear? GOOD afternoon!' and he slammed down the receiver with considerable force.

Then our Boats' Officer fixed me with a long blue stare and barked:

'What experience have you had on boats, Pierrepont?'

'Quite a lot, sir,' I stammered, and proceeded to give him a boastful and not particularly accurate account of my boating experience at *Tormentor*.

'You said you worked on a boat with a Kelvin engine?'

My knees began to shake as I admitted to having said so.

'Good! We'll soon see what sort of stuff you're made of! There's a 36-foot cutter with a Kelvin engine lying alongside the Royal Pier at this moment, and it's out of action because none of your lot can get the ruddy thing started; they're too busy sitting on their arses doing sweet Fanny Adams in the band-room. You get that engine going and one deck-hand who knows the sharp from the blunt end of a boat to come with you, and I'll let you have that boat to work on.'

My spirits rose at this challenge, but I had to wait another two days before I could get to grips with that boat as we worked in twenty-four-hour watches and I was off duty the following day.

It was a Sunday, and Margaret came round to Bridell Lodge early that morning to take me to church at the Seaman's Mission. It was a grand day, with fleecy white clouds sailing in convoy across a sky of purest azure blue. And the sound of those male voices singing in unison 'Eternal Father, strong to save' was so moving that I began to feel less sorry for myself and to discover that a squid was really quite an attractive amphibian after all!

Later that day I set my mind to the problem of finding another kindred spirit who was not averse to the idea of working on a boat. It was no use asking Anne, as they would not allow two stokers to work on the same boat together at *Squid*. There was one other girl who seemed different to all the others on the starboard watch, and it was quite clear that she was tired of sitting around in the band-room listening to obscene jokes. Her name was Joan Preece and she came from West Norwood in London. She was very small, with light brown hair that curled all over her head like a lamb's back and greenish speckled eyes which slanted upwards at the outer corners. She took life rather seriously and was inclined to indulge in a pessimistic outlook on many things, but she was a very hard and conscientious worker and loved the sea and boats with a real affection. And she was utterly fearless; the more a storm raged or the closer the bombs fell in an air-raid, the more Joan would laugh with the sheer exhilaration of dangerous living. She had been an Officer's Steward in the WRNS for a long time, and had loathed this job so much that a sympathetic Wren Officer at her last base had managed to arrange for her transfer to Boats' Crew. It was not long after her arrival at HMS *Squid*, that Joan was given the nickname of Winkle.

On the Monday afternoon Winkle and I escaped unnoticed from the band-room and set to work on the cutter with the Kelvin engine. It was in a filthy condition and we spent several hours scrubbing the decks and thwarts, cleaning out the bilges, mending the bilge pump and polishing all the brasswork. It was supper-time by then, and we felt it wiser to give evasive answers to the others, who showed a certain curiosity about our disappearance.

Next morning we were detailed off to carry endless sacks of potatoes round from B Shed at Town Quay to HMS *Gannet*, a job specially devised for us by the Wren in charge to keep us out of mischief. Having made the cutter shine and sparkle with soap and polish, we could hardly contain ourselves until we came on duty again. It would then be up to me to plumb the depths of my meagre knowledge and skill to get the engine running.

Twenty-four hours later Winkle and I were back in our boat again (already we had laid proprietory claims to her), and my brain felt like a vaporous whirlpool with all Chiefie's advice about engines fluttering round and round inside it. This business about treating them like human beings seemed to me of paramount importance, as a first step, for this one had obviously been neglected and maltreated over a long period.

Winkle cleaned down the outside of the engine with cotton-waste soaked in paraffin whilst I changed the oil in the sump, cleaned the jets in the carburettor, took the sparking-plugs to a garage to be sandblasted and examined the magneto with a morbid fascination. Electrics were a closed book to me, so I telephoned to Margaret at *Abatos* and she promised to meet me at the Guidlhall that night and unfold some of the mysteries of what induces an engine to spark. It turned out to be an uproarious evening, with half the crew of *Abatos*, as well as Lofty, inviting us to take the floor in quick succession. As a result I only gained some fragmentary hints about the interior of a magneto, and it was nearly the end of my first week at *Squid* before I considered the engine in a fit state to respond to the starting-handle. Winkle and I then proceeded to swing that handle until we were blue in the face; we primed the plugs and touched up their points with a pencil, we choked the carburettor and did just about everything except jump overboard. And suddenly it started! Just a feeble puttering chuff-chuff sort of noise to begin with, but when I opened up the throttle our Kelvin gave a good healthy roar, like a lion in a cage before feeding-time.

Winkle stood on her head, then turned several Catherine-wheels along the pier and, as luck would have it, Lt Sherwood appeared on the scene just then with a huge grin illuminating his rugged countenance. He hastily released the mooring-lines and took the tiller, whilst I engaged the clutch and Winkle bore away with the boat-hook. Like a band of rather furtive conspirators, we motored round the end of the pier and out towards the smiling waters on the southern horizon.

That day was a landmark in our existence at HMS *Squid*. From time to time there were setbacks in our sea-faring careers, but, on the whole, we never looked back for the next eighteen months to the dismal days of sitting around with nothing much to do during our working hours.

To begin with Lt Sherwood acted as our coxswain on the cutter, and Winkle and I became her official crew. We soon found that we were not the most popular Wrens in the bandroom, but this did not worry us particularly as there were so many exciting things happening in the big world outside.

Anne was one of the few other girls who owned a bicycle at *Squid*, and she and I used to cycle round the docks when we came off duty, watching the army embarking on the landing-craft. Southampton was seething with soldiers, tanks, guns and armoured vehicles by the middle of April, and they were continually being sent on mock invasions along the South Coast although no one knew when the real thing would be. Each day, when we cycled to and fro between the Royal Pier and Shirley, there were more and more ships up on the hards for loading, and more and more 'Pongos' wolf-whistling and catcalling as we came within range. Anne used to put her head down close to the handle-bars and pedal as hard as her legs would revolve, and I often had a hard struggle to keep up with her on these occasions.

About a week after we had started doing regular runs out to the ships in Southampton Water, Winkle and I came on duty one day to find that our Kelvin engine was no longer working; the Port Watch had managed to put it out of action the previous night. We ran to the boats' office, almost sobbing with anger and frustration, and it was not long before Lt Sherwood had arranged for two engineering Petty Officers to come round and examine the engine; but it took them a few days to diagnose and repair the damage, and those few days became a miserable gap in our lives. We were given all the dirtiest work to do in the band-room, whilst the usual unpleasant cackles came from the group around the stove. But Winkle was such a hard and energetic worker that she had often finished her job before anyone had time to devise another one for her. I, in contrast, used to move lethargically around the floor on my backside, seated on a duster covered in Mansion Polish, whilst Anne did *Petit Point*, curled up on one of the top bunks, and chattered away to us about her ponies and her favourite uncle who kept a beautiful donkey down in Cornwall.

All long leave had been stopped by then, and although my parents managed to get special police permits to come and visit me in Southampton one week-end, I was not allowed to travel to anywhere outside the military zone.

A week later our boat was ready for sea again and we went to work on her in earnest. A number of other boats had been allotted to HMS *Squid* by then, and Lt Sherwood was much too busy directing his little fleet from the boats' office to continue acting as our coxswain. Various Leading Wrens took charge of us, one by one, until he decided to make Winkle into the official coxswain of our boat as she was more reliable than any of the others, even if she hadn't yet achieved an anchor on her left arm.

April went out in a blaze of glory; but two days later it was blowing Force 9 from the south. Our Boats' Officer did not listen to weather forecasts or gaze up at the ragged grey clouds to foretell their sinister portents. He merely sat in his office issuing commonplace factual orders: 'Cutter Os will proceed to D Trot at 1100 hours. The Diesel launch will collect soldiers from landing-craft on A Trot... etc. etc.'

Some of the coxswains protested bitterly, but Winkle loved the rough seas and the challenge of handling a boat under such conditions; so we went on running however hard the wind blew, and there were certain things about those days which I shall never forget. A and B Trots were always the worst ones to visit in a southerly gale. They lay in the most exposed positions down at the far end of Southampton Water, and they often contained large merchant ships, destroyers and corvettes, as well as landing-craft.

On our last trip on May 2nd, we were sent down to A Trot to deliver five men aboard the *Empire Dockland*. It was a pitch black night with the wind screaming in the rigging like a thousand demented demons. Enormous white-crested waves reared up out of the blackness and crashed aboard our open cutter with an alarming frequency. The five sailors were huddled together up for'ard, trying to gain a little shelter from the high bows of the boat. It was nearly midnight when we reached A Trot and started our search for the *Empire Dockland*. Suddenly she loomed above us, a great mountain of a ship lying head-on to the gale, so that there was no lee side along which to approach her. We were about four feet away from the flimsy rope ladder on her starboard side when an immense wave lifted us up and up into the tempestuous night sky, until we were actually looking down on her deck for a few excruciating seconds; then the boat began to plunge downwards into a deep dark cavern, with a great deluge of water breaking over us like the Niagara Falls. Winkle clung to the tiller with a grip like a vice and our faithful Kelvin gasped and hissed, then ran on in a steady rhythm, holding the boat in slow ahead. The sailors did not wait for another seventh great wave to toss them in the air like autumn leaves; they jumped on to that rope ladder with the speed of grasshoppers and the last thing we heard as we drew away from the monstrous hull was the voice of the Belgian skipper, who was leaning far out over the bulwarks above us shouting into the gale: '*Nom d'une sacrée vache! Ce sont des femmes la bas, dans ce bateau!*'

Another night early in May, we had been to 2 and 3 Trots up the River Test and were on our way back when the air-raid warning sounded. We put on our tin helmets (mine had a picture of Popeye painted on the front by one of the seamen at *Tormentor*) and kept a good look-out all round us, as all the lights had been extinguished and it was another impenetrable black night with no moon or stars to guide us. Suddenly some anti-aircraft guns opened fire from near the end of the Ocean Dock, and by their light we saw the huge bulk of an unfinished section of Mulberry lying right across our path. There was just time to go full speed astern and then to navigate cautiously round the edge of it before the cloak of total darkness fell once more.

As the month of May advanced, so the number of ships increased and the tension born of too much waiting grew and grew. The last liberty-boats were usually packed with drunks and we began to take a morbid interest in dividing them into classes. There were the fighting drunks, usually the most difficult of all to cope with; the sleepy drunks, often a problem when it came to finding out which ships they belonged to; the amorous drunks, who sometimes needed very careful handling; and the happy generous drunks, our favourite category! The flow of language was quite impressive if a Yankee liberty-boat happened to venture too close to us, and those girls who had previously led a sheltered life found that their vocabularies were being increased at such a rate that they were scarcely able to absorb this strange new language.

Apart from the swear words, there were many other words used by the sailors which became part of our daily lives. To be chokka meant to feel fed up; gash was rubbish or waste food; elbow grease meant putting a bit of energy into whatever job one was doing; to be put in the rattle was to get into trouble; a bunting-tosser was a signalman; sparks was a radio operator; a bootneck was a Royal Marine, and a pongo was a soldier.

As we waited alongside the steps at Town Quay a few minutes before midnight, the flood gates would suddenly be opened by the duty sailor in the boats' office and eighty seamen would come tumbling down the steps, each one trying to be the first aboard our boat. Snatches of sentences reverberated against the dank and dripping harbour walls:

'Wotcher, Titch! Thought you was orff duty tenight. 'Ave a Mars Bar? Make yer grow, it will!'

'Coom over 'ere, Shiner, an' give me a pull oop. Ah've doon summat te ma leg an' Ah canna hardly move t'boogar.'

'Leave me alone yer perishin' shod. All I wan'sha bi' o' peash.'

'Hello, Stokes! If it ain't passionflower the engineer on tenight! 'Ow about comin' te the pichers wiv me temorrer? Bing Crosby's on up the Odeon.'

''Urry up, girls; lez git te 'ell aht of 'ere an' back te the ole floatin' coffin. Ah feel proper chokka tenight.'

And so it went on, night after night; soldiers and sailors all trying to forget that tomorrow might be their greatest day, or their last.

*   *   *

Ever since the dark days of the withdrawal from Dunkirk in 1940, the idea of an invasion of Europe by British soldiers had been germinating in the minds of a few far-sighted people. In the same year an organization called Combined Operations was founded, and their main preoccupation for the next three and a half years was to study and perfect the technique of landing on hostile coastlines. When Lord Louis Mountbatten was given the command of Combined Operations, some eighteen months later, he was instructed by Churchill to plan for the offensive.

By January 1943, with Russia and America as our allies, the prospect of an invasion of Europe in the foreseeable future became imminent. When Churchill and Roosevelt met in Casablanca that month, they agreed to appoint a joint staff to make definite plans for the invasion. It was during the six months following this meeting that the question of where to land in Europe was decided upon; a decision which remained a closely guarded secret until the day when the invasion actually took place. On the whole the Americans favoured Calais, although it was the most heavily defended area on the French seaboard; but their contention was that it offered the nearest and most direct route to Germany. However, the British Chiefs of Staff plumped emphatically for Normandy, because its defences were weaker and it could virtually be cut off from the rest of Europe by destroying the bridges over the Seine and Loire. In the end the British and American Chiefs of Staff reached an agreement over this, and at the conference in Quebec in August 1943 it was also decided that the Supreme Commander of all the forces should be American, his Deputy and his three Commanders-in-Chief should be British, and the invasion of Normandy should take place in May 1944.

Some months later, Roosevelt appointed General Eisenhower as the Supreme Commander of Operation Overlord, and he was directed to 'Undertake operations aimed at the heart of Germany and the destruction of her armed forces'. Air Chief Marshall Tedder was appointed as his Deputy Supreme Commander, and Admiral Ramsay, General Montgomery and Air Chief Marshall Leigh-Mallory to command the navies, armies and air forces of the Allied Expeditionary Force.

In November 1943 Churchill and Roosevelt met Stalin at a conference in Teheran, and he indicated quite clearly that he felt the British and Americans were not taking a fair share of the burden of fighting the Germans at that period. In order to allay his impatience, they promised Stalin that this state of affairs would soon be remedied.

In the meantime the German High Command, who had the strongest suspicions that plans for an invasion of Europe were being hurried forward, were divided amongst themselves as to how best to deal with it. Field Marshal Rommel, who was appointed to defend the coast of Europe at the end of 1943, started work at top speed to build fortifications all along what was known as the Atlantic Wall. He decided that Normandy was the most likely spot for the invasion, but Field Marshal von Rundstedt, who was his immediate superior, held different views. He was inclined to concentrate on reserve forces which he proposed to keep intact somewhere inland until after the invading force had actually landed. And he was convinced that the main landings would take place in the area surrounding Calais.

The Allies went to great pains to foster this deception. Whilst the main armies and fleets were being assembled in Hampshire and south-western England, enormous dummy. camps and dummy fleets of landing-craft were assembled in the neighbourhood of Dover. General Patton was brought back from the Mediterranean and officially put in charge of this army, with the maximum publicity attached to his appointment. But the British Secret Service was probably responsible, more than any other factor, for keeping this magnificent deception alive in the minds of the German High Command, and thereby increasing the confusion and disagreement which took place amongst their commanders. Even on D-Day itself, whilst the mighty invasion force was sailing across to Normandy, dummy fleets of ships and aircraft took off for Calais, using devices which made them appear twice as large on the enemy's radar screens. The deception was so successful that von Rundstedt, for one, kept his main reserves in the Calais area until several weeks after the landings on the Normandy coast, as he thought they were only a ruse and the main landings were still to come around Calais.

By May 1944 there were about a quarter of a million Allied troops and their equipment collected inside a narrow strip of coastline in southern England, and this area was sealed off from the rest of the country. By the middle of the month they had completed their long, arduous and often dangerous training, but none of them knew where they would be going, or when. The weather was perfect during most of May, but the men began to become bored and apprehensive, packed into their sealed camps with very little to do.

One of the reasons for the postponement of the invasion. until June was that there were still not enough landing-craft to transport the extra forces which Eisenhower had insisted on collecting. One more month of the highest possible speed of production in landing-craft was demanded, at the risk of Stalin's anger when the invasion had not started by the end of May, and the even greater risk of the whole secret being revealed.

*   *   *

During the first week in May Anne and I managed to get sleeping-out passes for one night when we were off duty, as long as we stayed inside the military zone. Directly after lunch that day we set off on our bicycles to go to her aunt's house at Cadnam in the New Forest. It was a grand day, grand day, with long golden sunbeams streaming through the young green foliage and long dark shadows reproducing the tall tranquil trees. We passed wild ponies grazing by the side of the road, and a band of gipsies clustered round a wood fire, their caravans grouped invitingly in the background.

Anne's aunt, Mrs. Dodgson, lived at Bartley Lodge, a mellow Georgian house the colour of a ripe peach, surrounded by a large garden where the fragrant smell of spring flowers assailed our unaccustomed nostrils with a most powerful and delightful odour. The same evening Mrs. Dodgson lent us a small pony-trap with which to explore the forest; the pony was called Rattles, and Anne and I took turns at driving him along the charming forest glades to Minstead and back. Drives like these through the New Forest were to sow the seeds of Anne's pony-driving career, at which she was later to become internationally famous.

The following evening was a sharp contrast. There was an air-raid warning early in the evening and we made a number of trips to D and E Trots through a thick smoke screen, with anti-aircraft guns firing all round us and the occasional sound of bombs exploding in the town.

After the midnight trip, Winkle, another girl and I went to bed aboard the Diesel launch, still wearing our tin helmets for some extraordinary reason. About half an hour later two incendiary bombs fell in the water, a few yards away from the end of the Royal Pier; our sleeping quarters leapt in the air like a startled mastodon, then settled back into the river with a heavy shower of flak cascading over the cabin-top. I remember that none of us felt particularly alarmed at the time, only excited by the perilous times we lived in. It was another matter when we were sent down into the underground shelter when we were off duty. There was one girl who invariably had hysterics, and it was always a question of whether someone would slap her face to stop her noise quickly, or whether we would all decide to indulge in screaming fits to keep her company!

A few nights after this raid, we were all asleep in the band-room when a messenger arrived on a motor-cycle with an urgent signal. The Diesel launch was to go to a ship on B Trot off Netley immediately, as there was a man having an epileptic fit on board and he must be taken to hospital without delay. A girl called Margaret Sparkes was ordered to go as coxswain, and Anne and I were to be her crew. It was 3 am, and Anne had done her coiffure with great care that night, having used an exceptionally large number of curlers to achieve the desired effect. There was another air-raid on, so she dressed rapidly and placed her tin helmet on top of all the curlers, and we set off into the dark tumultuous night. We soon found the ship and took the sick man across to Netley Hospital, but they refused to accept him as they had no free beds. We then brought him back to Town Quay and sent for an ambulance to take him to another hospital; it was daylight by the time we returned to HMS *Gannet*, and Anne removed all her curlers and brushed her hair out into a blonde fluffy halo of curls!

On Saturday, May 13th, Winkle and I were out on the River Test in our cutter, collecting men from the tank landing-craft on 2 and 3 Trots. Suddenly three immaculate RMLs swept past us, and standing on their bridges were Winston Churchill, Field Marshal Smuts and some of the Commonwealth Prime Ministers. They had come to inspect the invasion fleet, and it was an inspiring sight to see those great men at close quarters. I remember that Field Marshal Smuts stood as straight as a ramrod on the bridge of his vessel, with his hat planted fair and square above his stern face, and his gaze directed straight ahead of him, as if towards some promised land.

About this time there were many other ships in our lives, apart from the ever-increasing flotillas of landing-craft. We often ran trips to a sloop called the *Magpie*, a Polish cruiser, the *Conrad*, and a number of corvettes; *Campanula*, *Gentian* and *Potentilla*, and sometimes to the Greek corvettes *Tompazie* and *Armeria*. Then there were the army ships, manned by Royal Engineers: *Swift*, *Sir Walter Venning*, *Thames Coast*, *Talverne* and *Laguna Belle*. In complete contrast were the merchant ships which we visited regularly; the ones I remember best are the *Empire Dockland, Empire Russell, New Royal Lady, Antrim Coast, Twickenham Ferry, Hampton Ferry, Caverock, Maid of Orleans, Royal Daffodil, Saint Rule, Oceanway, Roebuck, Royal Ulsterman, Leviathan* and the *Sambur.*

There was one rather stout skipper who often came ashore in our boat and made a point of tipping us on his return journey, and trying to make dates in a husky whisper behind a newspaper, which was held aloft to shield his intentions from the common herd.

There were so many ships and people, but I think it was the little ships, the tugs, MFVs, balloon-boats and cutters run by the sailors from Town Quay, which became our greatest chummy ships. Diesel Launch No. 17 from Calshot was one of my favourites. Her coxswain, Joel Perkins, was a Cornish fisherman from St. Ives and a sea-dog of the old school. He was short, but powerfully built, with wiry brown hair, a rugged sun-tanned face and eyes of a certain shade of blue which hinted at the broad Atlantic rollers within the latitudes of the Trade Winds. He was inclined to be old-fashioned in his outlook, but Joel Perkins was always a good friend of ours and at times he radiated a special kind of wisdom which soothed our tired and muddled brains and created a strangely peaceful atmosphere around DL 17. Her crew consisted of three Scots: Peter Macdonald, a quiet brown-eyed sailor with a plum-red complexion, Robert Lobden, always known as 'Wee Jock', who had twinkling blue-grey eyes and a thousand wrinkles in his weather-beaten face; and Archibald Johnston, a young blonde stoker who took his work very seriously.

If ever there was an unpleasant job to be done, like taking a couple of drunk sailors who had missed the last liberty-boat back to their ship in the middle of the night, Joel Perkins would always ask Lt Sherwood if he could do it to save us going out again. DL 17 was a very gallant boat.

Another of our special favourites was the *Queen Boadicea*, a balloon-boat which used to be a Thames pleasure launch before the war. Every day she went out amongst the fleet, attached to a great silver barrage-balloon, and during an air-raid she and her sister ship the *Westcliffe Belle* were often responsible for protecting the landing-craft from the attentions of low-flying aircraft. Sometimes Winkle and I would go to sea in the *Queen Boadicea* during our afternoons off duty. We never seemed to have enough of the sea in those days, and a trip to the Isle of Wight and back on the *Duchess of Cornwall* or the *Solent Queen* was another of our favourite outings. These ships lay alongside the Royal Pier and Captain Larkin, the skipper of the *Duchess of Cornwall*, often let us take a turn at the wheel on the way across to Cowes.

As the month of May advanced, the pressure of work gradually increased and there came a time when we spent all our leisure hours sleeping on the grass in the garden at Bridell Lodge, and no longer felt inclined to go out dancing in the evenings. Bridell Lodge had belonged to a renowned spiritualist before the war, and he counted Conan Doyle as a member of his circle. The garden was liberally sprinkled with a gruesome medley of stone elephants and hippopotami, and there was even a replica of Stonehenge secreted behind the laurel bushes. A large hut in the garden had a wooden floor flamboyantly decorated with the signs of the zodiac.

On May 24th there was a fresh easterly wind blowing across Southampton Water and the midday sun was shining right into our eyes. Suddenly an exceptionally smart RML appeared in the path of the sun, coming towards us at a fair speed. Winkle altered course to starboard, and as the other vessel passed abeam of us we saw King George VI standing on the bridge, smiling and waving to his fleet.

The following afternoon we brought Lofty ashore in our boat. It was the first time I had seen him outside the Guildhall or the Seaman's Mission, and he suddenly confided to me that his name was Ernest and he came from Sussex! I was so taken aback by these unsolicited revelations that I just stared at him with my mouth wide open and forgot to put the gear lever in neutral when we reached Town Quay.

What with the King smiling at us the day before, and Lofty telling me his name at last, I thought that our days were numbered and the invasion of Europe must be very near indeed.

'Tarzan' (seaman on Tid 27).

HMS Gannet. (Where we live!)

The *Camel* up on the slips at Parson's Hard
with Su and Dottie underneath.

Di, Dottie and Sylvia under one of the
Conrad's guns in the Old Docks.

7

A Day to Remember

I T WAS JUNE 1st, and Tarzan was cooking spam fritters in the galley at HMS *Gannet*. Flaming June they called it, but the rain was beating down on the roof of the band-room and the wind rattled and shook the wooden framework like a tambourine solo.

Tarzan was a Lowestoft fisherman who had joined the navy for the duration, and found himself working as a seaman on a tug called *Tid 27*. He was immensely large and powerful, like a Siberian bear, with an abundance of brown hair which resisted the wind pressure with the sturdy defiance of a wire scrubbing-brush, and a red face framed by a splendid chestnut-coloured beard in which a couple of pigeons might have nested without being noticed. Inside this striking exterior lived a very shy and kind-hearted person. He was an old friend of one of the nicest coxswains on the Starboard Watch a girl called Joan Horton who came from Walton-on-the-Naze.

Everyone was pleased to see Tarzan whenever he came round to HMS *Gannet*, and he used to make it his second home. Many a time we would return from a cold exhausting trip, with only twenty minutes to spare before we were due to start off again, and Tarzan would be standing in the galley putting the finishing touches to a tasty meal which he had specially prepared for us.

On that evening of June 1st, Winkle and I were sitting on the floor in a corner of the band-room, cleaning the navigation. lamps and filling them with paraffin ready for the night ahead of us. That daily ritual of preparing our lamps was something which I loved in those days; the polishing of the reflectors and the glass with clean handfuls of cotton-waste, the intoxicating smell of paraffin which we usually contrived to spill on the floor, and then the clear beautiful glow of the port and starboard lights as we lit them to see if their wicks needed trimming.

Tarzan put his head out of the galley and shouted 'Wakey, wakey; rise and shine!' through the open cabin door, where half a dozen girls were snatching a few minutes rest in between trips. In a matter of seconds twelve hungry 'gannets' were seated round the long deal table, with Tarzan standing at the head dishing out generous helpings of spam fritters and baked beans, and large mugs of scalding black tea. Tarzan always acted as mother when he was there, and that night was something of an occasion as we were to have afters, a rare event when we were on duty. The afters were several basketfuls of luscious dark red strawberries which First Officer Butters, the senior Wren Officer at HMS *Squid* had made a special journey down to the Royal Pier to deliver to us that morning. Such delightful gifts from our superiors were not an everyday occurrence in those days; it was just that this was rather a special week in our lives.

It had all started the previous Tuesday with a lecture on security from the Captain of HMS *Squid*; the Boats' Crew Wrens and the sailors who worked from B Shed round at Town Quay were his particular target. After impressing upon us the infinite dangers involved in so much as opening our mouths or inhaling through our noses amongst strangers, he proceeded to tell us that there would be no more shore leave from then onwards and we should all be confined to barracks at the end of the Royal Pier, completely devoid of any contact with the outside world. All phone calls were forbidden and it was no use writing letters home as there was no postal service working inside the military zone. We were given exactly two hours to return to Bridell Lodge, collect as many of our personal belongings as we wanted, and report back to Lt Sherwood's office at the end of Town Quay.

An afternoon of sheer chaos resulted from this order. Both the Port and Starboard Watches, who normally only met at midday during the change of the watch, arrived at Bridell Lodge simultaneously and descended upon the Boats' Crew cabin like a swarm of hungry locusts. The contents of drawers and cupboards, bedding, photographs, gasmasks and a hundred other personal possessions were emptied into one huge pile in the middle of the floor, and it was then a question of the survival of the fittest! An hour later the whole place was stripped bare; even the roll of lavatory paper had disappeared from its holder in the bathroom. No one knew how long we were going for, but the spirit of self-preservation and laying in stocks for a siege flourished mightily.

By four o'clock that afternoon there appeared to be a nomadic encampment outside the boats' office and Lt Sherwood, who was also feeling the pressure of fast-moving events, glared at us through his office window with Arctic blue eyes, then came to the door and roared, 'What the ruddy hell d'you think this place is? A flaming gipsy's camp in the New Forest? Get all that gear out of my sight before I burst a blood vessel!'

The colour of his face gave due warning that he might well do so at any moment, so we shouldered all our worldly possessions like a string of baggage mules and set off towards the Royal Pier. A battalion of the Royal Tank Regiment was trundling along the main road just then, and we were urged forward by a chorus of injunctions from the Pongos...

'Git a move on there, girls! You ain't got all day te git there!'

'Whatcher, Shortie! Movin' 'ouse, are yer? Got kicked aht by the ole man ah shouldn't wonder?'

'Look at them bits o' fluff in bell-bottom trarsers, Nobby! Look more like bleedin' refugees te me. 'Ow abaht shiftin' their gear in our lorry, Sarge?'

Thanks to the army we reached the Royal Pier in double quick time. We passed through the big iron gates and the small iron turnstiles carrying our mountain of luggage, then the gates were firmly locked behind us and that was that.

All that happened two days before. By Thursday, June 1st, we had begun to enjoy our enforced imprisonment, and it seemed to us that there would have been no point in roaming round the town in the evenings as the most exciting things in the whole world were taking place right in front of our eyes.

There was a little black tug called the *Chokka* which worked from the Royal Pier, and spent all day and most of the night helping us on the ammunition runs. Most of the landing-craft had taken aboard their quota of soldiers, tanks, guns and armoured cars by then, and they were back on their moorings as sealed ships. No men were allowed ashore, and our job was to deliver extra ammunition and urgent signals at all hours of the day and night.

Late that evening there was a pause; no more boxes waiting for delivery and no more signals for the time being. Winkle and I moored our boat alongside the *Chokka* and climbed aboard to drink hot chocolate on the after deck. The new moon was shining fitfully through banks of long black clouds the shape of racing-cars. We sat around the towing-winches on coils of hemp and manilla, and we were all so tired that we just sat there and sipped away at our chocolate in silence. There was Frank, the coxswain, a small man with sharp features who drew beautiful pictures and had a never-failing sense of humour. Then there was Bryn, the Welsh seaman with a little boy's expression on his dirty face and laughing eyes which sparkled like a sunlit mountain pool. Alf, the stoker, also came from South Wales, and his whole being was filled with the essence of pure music, the heritage of his native land. And, last but not least, was the old engineering Petty Officer who sat on the hatch cover puffing away at a vile mixture of Old Holborn and old socks in the bowl of his pipe, the picture of a man who was entirely contented with his lot.

Suddenly Alf looked up at the new moon and began to sing. Bryn joined him and they sang some of the ancient Gaelic songs of their homeland and the melodies were so beautiful that I wanted to howl. Next they sang 'The White Cliffs of Dover', and we all began to sing. Then a strange thing happened; all at once there were hundreds of voices, basses, baritones, tenors, contraltos, sopranos, all singing 'There'll be bluebirds over, the white cliffs of Dover: Tomorrow, just you wait and see...' No one felt like sleeping on that long restless night so they lifted up their hearts and sang, and a million miles away the stars looked down compassionately and the crescent moon shone with a special radiance upon the puny mortals, waiting endlessly for they knew not what.

*   *   *

By June 1st all the final preparations for the invasion of Europe were completed, and a team of meteorologists had been assembled to predict one of the most important weather forecasts ever made.

There were only three possible days at the beginning of June, the 5th, 6th, or 7th, when all the factors like the state of the tides and the moon would be just right for launching Operation Overlord, and it was absolutely essential to have reasonably calm and clear weather for the landings on the coast of Normandy. During most of May the weather had been exceptionally good, but on June 1st it suddenly turned dull and grey. The following morning the meteorologists reported a complex system of three depressions moving in fast from the Atlantic. By June 3rd the team forecast high winds, low cloud and poor visibility for the next few days.

Eisenhower, when he heard this forecast, immediately called a conference at Southwick House with his deputy, his three Commanders-in-Chief and their Chiefs of Staff. There were nine men in all; two of them Americans and seven British. But the ultimate decision and responsibility rested on Eisenhower himself, and whatever he decided, either way, might end in disaster.

Already many of the larger ships had sailed from Scotland and Northern Ireland, and a quarter of a million troops and their equipment were cooped up in considerable discomfort aboard the landing-craft and transports; the camps they had left were being filled by reserve troops, and there were 4,900 fighters and 5,800 bombers ready to take off at a moment's notice in support of the invasion. The great problem which only Eisenhower could decide, was whether to stop the whole gigantic machine, which had already been put in motion, for twenty-four hours, or whether to let it go on.

At that first momentous meeting of the Chiefs of Staff on the Saturday evening, June 3rd, the sky above Southwick House was quite clear and there was only a gentle zephyr fluttering the leaves on the trees. This must have made Eisenhower's decision twice as hard; however he postponed his final judgement of the situation and arranged to hold another meeting at 4.30 am the following day.

On Sunday, June 4th, the forecast was just as bad, although the weather in Hampshire appeared equally good. Already some of the American landing-craft had sailed from harbours in South Devon and Cornwall, and were on their way up-Channel to the great rendezvous south of the Isle of Wight.

At that Sunday morning meeting the Chiefs of Staff were vehemently divided in their opinions. Montgomery, in particular, was willing to go ahead with the invasion at once; but Eisenhower decided to postpone Operation Overlord for twenty-four hours and to recall the ships already at sea. During the morning the wind rose to gale force and there was a chaotic scene at Portland where all the American landing-craft from south-west England tried to enter the harbour which was already crammed full of ships. However, by the evening order had been restored, and Eisenhower was once more faced with the terrible decision of whether the invasion should be launched or not. By then the weather outside Southwick House was visibly impossible, but the team of meteorologists offered a faint chance of a temporary improvement by Tuesday morning. Eisenhower knew that if the invasion was postponed for a further two weeks, until the tides were right again, the chances were that it might never take place. The men could not be kept aboard their ships for that length of time, and already they had been briefed about the places where they were to land. How could the secret possibly be kept, if tens of thousands of men were let loose in England for two weeks.

The final meeting took place on Monday, June 5th, at 4 am, when Eisenhower uttered the few heroic words which altered the whole course of history. 'OK. We'll go,' was all he said. Operation Overlord was under way.

*   *   *

By the Sunday evening, June 4th, we had been working almost non-stop for five days. There were no longer two watches, each working for twenty-four hours, or crews of three for each boat. We were all hard at it at the same time, often on different boats or with different crews to those we normally worked with.

I was acting as stoker and deck-hand on a new cutter under a Leading Wren called Ena Groves. She came from Solihull near Birmingham, her age was twenty-one and she was built on a miniature scale. She had a pretty little face illuminated by the brightest brown eyes, and she was a very dashing coxswain who always approached her targets at full speed and often took enormous risks. Ena was extremely popular amongst the officers on the landing-craft, and she often received invitations to parties in the wardrooms. I liked her well enough ashore, but at sea it was another matter. Like many small people, she was apt to become rather bossy as soon as the mooring-lines were released from the shore, and she always assumed that I would do the wrong thing on a boat which caused her to shout at me incessantly.

However, by Sunday evening we were both so tired that we had a hard job to keep going, and we had reached a state of tolerant neutrality in our relationship afloat.

The wind had been rising all day and heavy showers of driving rain mingled with the flying spindrift, contriving to form a scene of grey and gloomy desolation. Thousands of men sat huddled together under the broad sea-green camouflage nets which covered them and their equipment. There were no smiles or jokes that day; the whole world seemed to be enclosed inside a padded cell, a sort of grey-green sepulchre; and the silence was only relieved, from time to time, by the dismal howling of the wind in the rigging of ten thousand ships.

There was a pair of tank landing-craft, numbers 474 and 7011, moored on B Trot off Netley, and they had not yet been ordered in to the hard to load their quota of men and tanks. Ena was on very friendly terms with George and Henry, the two young lieutenants who commanded them, and late on Sunday evening they invited us to come aboard for supper. We had lost all count of time and could not remember when we had last had a square meal, so we accepted their invitation with pleasure. The wind was blowing gale force by then and it was too dangerous to moor our cutter alongside the landing-craft in such an exposed position, so Ena arranged for us to be dropped and picked up later by one of the other Wren's cutters.

Sometime during the early hours of Monday morning we sat down to a banquet of fried eggs, bacon, sausages and baked beans piled on top of gargantuan slices of fried bread. The wardroom on LCT 7011 was as warm and snug as a thrush's nest and the whole scene had a dreamlike quality about it which I shall never forget. Ena was chattering away happily to George and Henry, and I had a large sausage poised on the end of a fork, half-way between the plate and my mouth which was wide open to receive it, when there was an imperious knocking at the door.

'Come in!' shouted Henry, and we saw Sparks, the wireless operator, standing there, his expression a curious mixture of exaltation and impending doom.

'Urgent signal just come through, sir,' he announced. Both ships to go in to the hard for loading immediately. Then we've got sailing orders for 0600 hours.'

For a few brief seconds there was a pregnant silence... So this was it; the invasion of Europe was about to commence... Then the two ships burst into rumbustious vibrant life. Orders were shouted, heavy boots clattered along the iron decks, engines began to throb in the bowels of both ships, mooring-lines were cast off and suddenly we were under way.

Ena and I had no time to worry about what would become of us. My dearest wish at that moment, was to remain aboard LCT 7011 and to take part in the landings on the Normandy coast.

In the bitterly cold hour before dawn, Ena and I stood on the bridge of our LCT as she motored along Southampton Water. The night was full of passing shadows, phantom ships on the move, all stealing silently through the night down to the open sea.

All too soon we reached the main loading hard close to Town Quay. The ramp was dropped and we could see a large group of wan-faced soldiers waiting patiently near their tanks. The whole place was swarming with military police, so George decided that we had better go ashore disguised as men, otherwise we should all be in the rattle.

Ena and I hastily pinned up our hair and concealed it under our host's caps, then we donned their long watch-coats and set off down the ramp and across the hard at a fair speed. All around us the men had started to move towards their ships and we passed through the khaki throng unnoticed. It was 4.30 am on the morning of D-Day-1.

Four hours later I awoke from a deep dreamless sleep to find that someone was squeezing a spongeful of ice-cold water over my face. A signal had just come through from the boats' office to say that all of us were wanted round at Town Quay immediately. I had not bothered to undress that night, so it took no more than a couple of minutes to pull on my sea-boots and duffel-coat, brush my hair and ram a cap down on top of it Ten minutes later we were lined up in front of Horace Sherwood, listening to what he had in store for us.

'There are three personnel landing-craft which have broken down somewhere near the Needles,' he told us. 'And I'm sending you girls down there on the *Chokka* to bring them back. I know that some of you would rather stow away on a ship that's bound for France, but the navy won't allow that and this is the best I can do for you!'

At 10 am we were all aboard the *Chokka*, steaming down the River Test towards Southampton Water. Although the wind was no longer blowing gale force there was plenty of it, and we were soaked to the skin before we had gone very far Presently the sun came out and Frank, the coxswain, let Winkle and I and some of the others steer the tug in turns. Bryn Hatch was down in the galley making cocoa, and from the open cover above the engine-room came the clear beautiful notes of Alf's voice, singing 'Roses of Picardy', and a thin spiral of pungent smoke from the PO's pipe.

All around us the great armada was on the move. There were all the ships we knew so well: the Force Pluto ships from *Abatos*, the infantry landing-craft from *Tormentor*, all the hundreds of tank landing-craft from Southampton; K Squadron, N Squadron, the Mark Vs and D15 Flotilla; so many of our favourite ships, all flying barrage-balloons, like silver bumble-bees sailing amongst the fast-moving clouds. Then there were the armed merchant cruisers, destroyers, minesweepers, corvettes, trawlers and ocean tugs, every one of them moving southwards towards Normandy and a fate unknown.

At last the great day had come; the tension was broken and the soldiers and sailors laughed and cheered as our little tug kept pace with them, clouds of rainbow-tinted spray breaking over her stubborn black bows. One man leant over the stern of his landing-craft as it gathered way and called out to us: 'You're the last bit of Old England we'll see for a while, girls, and you sure look worth fighting for!'

Out beyond the Needles the great west wind was still blowing lustily and stalwart companies of white-capped waves advanced up the Channel, singing a boisterous song as they broke against the ancient shores of England.

As we turned for home with our three forlorn landing-craft in tow, we could still see a thousand grey dots on the southern horizon. Sometimes they merged together into one gigantic grey dot, or perhaps it just seemed that way because of the misty curtain which would persist in falling in front of our eyes.

PO Gwen and Micky on top of the wheelhouse of the Diesel.

Tommy on the Diesel with Gwen coxing.

LCT 960 (and part of 1109) on 2 Trot.

Crew of LCT 960. Left to Right:

Back row: Skipper, Mac, Baldy, Tubby, Jock, Bevin, Gipsy, No 1. (Jimmy!)

Front row: Harry, Wee George, Guns, Coxsun.

8

The Bridgehead into Europe

UTAH, OMAHA, GOLD, Juno and Sword... Those were the code names of the five famous beaches strung out along the coast of Normandy where the Allied Expeditionary Forces landed on D-Day, June 6th, 1944. It was, perhaps, the greatest amphibious military undertaking in the whole of history.

The five assault forces had embarked in over four thousand ships at twelve different ports along the south coast of England, and this mighty fleet had assembled, on June 5th, at a rendezvous south of the Isle of Wight. Minesweepers cleared channels through the extensive minefields, and a thousand other warships escorted the armada across to Normandy and supported the landings with their gunfire.

By D-Day the Allies had achieved complete control in the air, and not one of their huge force of over ten thousand fighters and bombers fell to the Luftwaffe. Before the invasion started the Allied Air Forces had been waging a scientific bombing campaign against the most vital German lines of communication, which included the main French railway network and marshalling yards. The result of this was to hamper all the German preparations to meet an invasion when the time came, and to create a chaotic hold-up of troops and equipment behind the coastal defences.

Following the airborne landings to secure the flanks of the armies, the Americans landed on Utah and Omaha beaches on the east side of the Cherbourg peninsula, and the British and Canadians landed on Gold, Juno and Sword beaches in the province of Calvados. The first American objective was to secure a base from which, eventually, to capture the important port of Cherbourg. The American 4th Division landed on Utah Beach with comparatively few losses, but on Omaha Beach they were less fortunate; bad launchings combined with poor air support contrived to pin the 1st Division to the beach for most of the day, and they suffered three thousand casualties.

Farther east, the British and Canadians had been instructed to capture the towns of Bayeux and Caen and the road which linked them. Although they failed to achieve these objectives on D-Day itself, by midnight the bridgehead into Europe had been secured and the Allies had won the battle of the beaches.

The Germans were still convinced that the main Allied assault was yet to come in the neighbourhood of Calais, so ingenious had been our deception. They were almost devoid of air power by then, and the Atlantic Wall was still unfinished. Only the 21st Panzer Division, which held the British outside Caen, gave any indication of the formidable military strength of the Hun.

There were 11,000 casualties in all amongst the Allied forces on D-Day; 2,500 had died out of more than 156,000 who landed in Normandy.

Once the first thrilling news of the invasion had been received and absorbed by all of us in Southampton, a period of waiting ensued which was enshrouded in a grey blanket of depression. Up and down Southampton Water the mooring-buoys bowed and curtsied to the flood and ebb, the only physical objects in sight on that long monotonous stretch of water. All the ships that used to swing to those buoys, all our favourite ships and the ones we did not care for so well and our tea, chocolate and rum ships had gone, and no one knew if or when they would ever return.

We scrubbed and polished our boat until it shone like an oriental sunrise. I drained the oil out of the sump and filled it with fresh oil, cleaned the plugs and carburettor and did a few other maintenance jobs on the engine. We returned to Bridell Lodge in Shirley next afternoon and immersed ourselves in vast piles of dhobying, but to do any of these things required an enormous effort of will-power, as a lethargy born of too little sleep and a sense of unutterable anticlimax had gripped us in its powerful embrace.

Three days later we were jerked out of our selfish brooding by a scene which I shall never forget. An armed merchant ship came alongside the Royal Pier and several hundreds of German prisoners disembarked from her under the supervision of a strong military escort. We stood outside the band-room watching them as they shambled down the gangway and lined up along the whole length of the pier. I am not sure what I had expected to see, but in that precise moment I suddenly became aware of the indescribable tragedy and horror of war. These were no proud and noble specimens of the Aryan race, but a pathetic collection of under-fed, tired and ill-looking youths wearing the ragged remains of their uniforms, with a forlorn and hopeless look in their eyes which made it impossible to view them objectively as the dreaded Huns, the greatest enemies of the human race.

Last of all a mangy black mongrel came down the gangway, one more bit of flotsam and jetsam in the tide of war; he trotted up to one of the prisoners and fixed him with a look of such single-minded devotion that I almost burst into tears when the wretched beast was hustled into a police van and the black doors shut irrevocably behind him.

An order was given at the far end of the pier and the hordes began to move. Many of them were wounded and the stretcher-cases were carried by those who were strongest amongst them. A great silence seemed to fall on the dock area in Southampton, broken only by the shuffling footsteps of hundreds of miserable Huns.

The following day more ships came alongside the pier to unload their cargoes of wounded British soldiers, and the only thing which relieved the horror of that day was an inspection of our quarters by Superintendent Curtis. No doubt all the preparation involved for this event was specially designed to keep our minds and eyes off the unhappy scenes around us.

On June 11th Maureen came over from *Tormentor* to visit me, and when I had finished work at midday we cycled across to Woolston to call on Margaret. She had been moved from the South-Western Hotel into a new house with a fine view over Southampton Water and she was doing secretarial work at *Abatos* just then, as *Anndora* had broken down once more. Maureen and I were careful to express no sympathy, as Margaret was as fiercely loyal to Force Pluto as ever; but the three of us were glad to be together again for a few hours in which we could forget the war and talk of cabbages and kings and a number of other frivolous things.

As the month of June advanced, many of our ships began to trickle back to Southampton. Amongst the tank landing-craft it was a familiar sight to see the stern half of the ship towing the bows behind it along Southampton Water.

George and Henry's ships, 474 and 7011, both returned in one piece, and their skippers brought for us a varied selection of trophies in the shape of German cap badges, an iron cross, some photographs found in a dead German's wallet and a number of mouth-organs and concertinas. The memory of the first batch of prisoners was still too vivid to allow me to receive my share of the loot with much pleasure, but I hid it away in a corner of the band-room, almost afraid to touch it, much to the amusement of some of the others.

Every day more and more lorry-loads of Americans arrived in Southampton and embarked on the landing-craft which had returned from Normandy to fetch them. The second wave of reinforcements crossed the Channel and landed in France, whilst the Allied Expeditionary Force continued to advance towards Paris.

By the end of the month most of the trots were full of ships again and we were running non-stop, ferrying men, stores and signals to and fro in our boat. Winkle and I became so tired that we spent much of our time off duty asleep in the garden at Bridell Lodge, or sitting around on the *Chokka* listening to Alf and Bryn singing, drinking endless mugs of tea and darning socks for the crew.

The corvette *Campanula* came back from France and there was a night at the end of June which I remember vividly. It was blowing great guns from the south-west and the moon was shining fitfully through ragged black clouds as we pounded down Southampton Water, our boats filled to overflowing with liberty men from the corvette. Someone began to sing 'Roll out the Barrel', and soon there were seventy or eighty sailors singing, their voices mingling with the song of the wind and the breaking waves which drenched us all with spray. The whole world seemed to belong to us on a night like that, and all the tiredness and confusing thoughts drained away in the immediate glory of our surroundings.

Maureen's boy-friend, Eric, had suddenly arrived home on leave from Algiers at the end of June, and he and Maureen were married a week later. I was on duty that afternoon and could not go to their wedding which was a bitter disappointment.

About this time our boat began to develop frequent engine trouble, and I felt less and less well due to lack of sleep, irregular meals and spending hours in soaking clothes whilst on duty. For once I was really delighted to go home on ten days' leave towards the end of July.

On this occasion I luxuriated in having breakfast on a tray in bed, going for long walks in the country with my parents and generally being made a fuss of by old friends whose existence I had almost forgotten. My mother arranged a few parties for my benefit in the evenings, as she was obsessed with the idea that I was meeting a large number of unsuitable men in Southampton and it was her duty to counteract this hazard by every means at her disposal. It so happened that the most promising means that particular week was a South African naval officer from the cruiser *Emerald*, with whom my father had played bridge at the Junior Carlton Club the previous week. He was a young man of florid complexion and pale blue eyes, which glinted with the same hard intensity as pellets of ice on a northern glacier. Tufts of gingerish hair sprouted from his cheeks in what is known in the navy as 'bugger's grips', and he exuded an alarming aura of lusty and exuberant vitality which he assured me was a common feature of people from the New World. By the end of that week I felt like the last stronghold in decadent old England, willing to die, if need be, to keep it that way for ever and ever!

On the final day of my leave I went for a long country walk with my father and we were chased by a herd of cows and forced to climb into the branches of an oak tree and wait there until they had dispersed. Any countryman will tell you that such a thing cannot happen, for cows are friendly beasts and they will do no more than cluster around you and nuzzle you out of curiosity. Be that as it may, these cows advanced on us at a brisk canter, shaking their horns in a menacing manner, and my father and I, being Londoners at heart, took immediate avoiding action by climbing the nearest tree in sight!

When I returned to Southampton at the end of July I found that Anne had been taken into sick-bay with pneumonia and was seriously ill. It took her a long time to recover and it was the end of her career in the WRNS, as she was invalided out of the service later on that autumn. Winkle and I were very sorry to lose a good friend.

August arrived in a blaze of sunshine and it was a pleasure to be afloat in such grand weather. Our boat skimmed across the glittering dancing wavelets with a new and vibrant rhythm, and the landing-craft of the Shuttle Service came and went between England and Normandy with a reassuring regularity. Meanwhile the Force Pluto ships were kept equally busy running to Arromanches and back, making sure that the Allied Expeditionary Force was supplied with fuel.

On August 11th all the Boats' Crew Wrens at HMS *Squid* were moved into new quarters in the Royal Hotel in the centre of Southampton, a privilege which we took some while to appreciate. Over the months we had become quite fond of Bridell Lodge, and the night before leaving there we gave a farewell party. Each girl was allowed to ask one guest, and the entertainment included beer, fish and chips, and dancing to an ancient gramophone in the garden hut, the décor of which was supposed to resemble an intimate Italian night-club lit by candles stuck in Chianti bottles. Lt Sherwood and all the sailors who worked in the boats' office and on the boats running from Town Quay were included. amongst the guests, and one of them, who was always known as 'Blossom' on account of his delicate pink complexion, arrived bearing a gift of a bottle of rum which was received with enthusiasm by all present. A Wren officer had been detailed off to keep an eye on things and generally act as chaperone for the evening, and she and Horace Sherwood took to the floor early on and executed an intricate *pas se doble* to the admiration of all the audience.

After a slightly sticky beginning the party soon got under way and everyone began to enjoy themselves according to their various tastes. Tarzan sat in a corner wearing a pea-green admiral's hat and sipping a pint of bitter with appreciative smacking noises; Winkle performed a ballet solo in the middle of the floor, until she was partnered by Blossom who acted as an accompanying gigolo; some Royal Marines, who had been invited by our Leading Wren and her clique, started a violent argument with a group of sailors and began to trace their opponent's ancestry in loud braying voices and singularly unflattering terms; the crews of the *Chokka* and Diesel Launch 17 sang harmoniously in a corner together, and Lt Sherwood surveyed his flock benignly as he lifted his elbow with a steady rhythm and beat time to the music with a fork on a biscuit tin. Sometime around 2 am it occurred to me that it was one of the most splendid parties I had ever been to!

The fine summer weather continued and Winkle and I discovered a most enjoyable way to spend our off-duty hours. We would take our bicycles across on the ferry to Hythe and ride through a forest of tall pine trees to Lepe, where we could swim in clear blue salty water instead of the brown oily liquid which passed as sea water in Southampton. The beach at Lepe was a grand place to spend a summer's afternoon, and on our way home we would often stop at a little cottage surrounded by blue hydrangeas where teas, which included home-made scones and strawberry jam, were served in a room with a low oak-beamed ceiling and a huge inglenook fireplace. The striking contrast between these peaceful rural surroundings and the perpetual roar of tanks and armoured vehicles passing through Southampton on their way to the loading hards was a constant source of wonder and bewilderment.

One night during the middle of August Winkle's home in London was bombed. Fortunately her parents escaped unhurt, and she was given a few days' compassionate leave to go to their assistance. During her absence I worked with one of the other coxswains who allowed me to take the tiller for several hours each day and even to bring the boat alongside ships at night. The first thrill, which I had experienced at *Tormentor*, of holding that magic piece of wood and sawing it to and fro according to my whim, had if anything increased as time went by, and I used to stand on the stern thwart of our cutter, puffed up with as much pride and self-satisfaction as a royal peacock, oblivious to the succinct remarks which came from the for'ard half of the boat:

"Old tight, mates! Git ready te abandon ship. There's Stokes at the 'elm today!'

'Ah'm goin' te put in a complint, ah am. Perishin' engineers tikin' charge o' this valuable cargo! An' ah ain't even tiken aht me life policy.'

'Give over, Blondie! My mum won't arf sort you aht if 'er one an' only don't never see Civvy Street no more.'

It was about this time that the Allied Expeditionary Force reached Paris and the city finally liberated itself from the German yoke.

*   *   *

During that summer a girl called Susan Huish joined our crew as deck-hand, having worked before with Ena Groves for some months. She was a tall blonde with a face like a Florentine Madonna, and enormous eyes the size of ping-pong balls and the colour of cabochon sapphires. She came from a village near Winchester called Micheldever, where her mother lived in a charming old-world cottage. For nearly a year Winkle, Sue and I were to remain together in the same crew, and we all found it a very happy arrangement.

Early on in our acquaintance the three of us decided that one of the pleasantest ways of spending our afternoons off duty was to go to sea in other boats whenever the time permitted. In mid-September we had a memorable voyage on a little tug known as *Laurea*, or the MN Mail Boat, which carried the mail to all the merchant ships in the Southampton area, and a good many naval ships as well. The crew had characteristic naval nicknames... Taffy, Half-Pint, Airtrigger and Stokes, the latter being a boy from Grimsby with an untidy mop of black hair, sad grey eyes and a heart of gold; he insisted on buying us a luscious bunch of grapes nearly every day that summer, and he would present them at the band-room door with a princely dignity when he came off duty.

The MN Mail Boat was one of the most popular boats on Southampton Water, and, by nature of its calling, was always assured of a royal welcome alongside any ship. On the day when Winkle, Sue and I went to sea in her we visited ships at anchor off Ryde, Cowes and Yarmouth, and everywhere we were greeted by smiling faces, mugs of tea and tots of rum in exchange for the mail bags which we distributed amongst the fleet like millionaires distributing largesse.

Another voyage we made was on the *Queen Boadicea*, taking a barrage-balloon to a ship which was waiting for us near the Needles. That was a much quieter affair, but it was almost dark by the time we turned for home. The stars came out, one by one, against a background of royal-blue velvet, and suddenly I saw, for the first time in my life, two shooting stars flashing across the brilliant starry firmament. The water was full of phosphorescence that night; a hundred thousand glittering emeralds danced along the crest of our bow-wave and curved away in sinuous lines into the dark waters astern. Sometimes I used to sit on the bows of a boat on a night of such exquisite beauty and feel almost dizzy with a ridiculous sort of unquestioning happiness. There were no thoughts for the past or future, the only reality was NOW; that inexpressibly glorious and unforgettable moment in time, when the whole world seemed to stop revolving on its axis, so rapt was it in the sheer wonder of existence.

As the autumn advanced and the days drew in, a tougher sterner element began to creep into our lives. The wrath of Poseidon returned with the equinoctial gales, and the strength of the wind was so great that we had to move all our boats round to Town Quay at 5 am one morning, to prevent them being smashed alongside the Royal Pier. A period of clammy grey fogs ensued, a trying time for all the coxswains who were hard put to it not to run aground on the Gymp or any of the other mudbanks.

At the beginning of October my mother and father came to stay in Southampton for a few days, and our boat was put on the slips for a thorough overhaul at the same time. I found myself leading a life of extraordinary contrasts, a type of double life which had its serious complications. There would be formal dinners at the Polygon Hotel (my parents always changed for dinner whatever the circumstances), followed by an evening playing bridge or chess in the lounge or going to a symphony concert at the Guildhall. Early the following morning I would be attired in filthy dungarees, lying on the wet oily slipway scraping barnacles off the bottom of our cutter, at the same time trying to hold my own against the parties of naval onlookers who came to offer us advice at frequent intervals. Every day Lt Sherwood walked round from the boats' office to inspect our efforts and to praise the results if he saw any signs of our spirits flagging. It was the first time that any of us had scraped and repainted a boat before and it was a curiously fascinating task, getting to know every inch of the hull, much of which was normally under water, repairing the blemished woodwork, sandpapering it down to a smooth even surface, and then the thrill of repainting the whole boat and standing back with pride to admire one's handiwork. Because there was no means of lifting the boat on to a proper cradle or chocks, we had to lie on the slipway most of the time, working upside-down, with large blobs of grey paint landing on our faces and in our hair whenever the brush was overloaded, and meandering streams of it flowing gently up our arms from the wrists to the arm-pits. By the end of the day it was a real effort to present a clean and respectable appearance amongst the old ladies and senior naval officers who frequented the Polygon Hotel.

On my parents' last evening in Southampton we went for a stroll down the main street towards the Bargate and I suddenly noticed, with qualms of misgiving, a group of cheerful-looking sailors advancing towards us on the far side of the street, the crew of one of our favourite tea and rum ships, LCT 960. Dominating the group was a tall Scottish signalman, Harry McDade, who had brown curly hair, merry blue eyes and a self-assurance and special brand of humour which carried him along through many scrapes and tight corners, always floating on a cloud a few inches above the ground. The moment Harry, or Bunts as he was usually known, spotted me he sized up the situation in the fluttering of an eyelid and determined to add to my discomfiture by a good leg-pull.

'Och look, Tubby!' Bunts advised his mate in a hoarse whisper which carried as far as the Civic Centre. ''Tisna tha' our ain puir wee stoker fra' the Cotter 08? Juist the lassie Ah had it on the tip o' ma tongue to ask along for a wee dram at the Blue Boar tonight!'

A look of fierce bewilderment spread across my mother's countenance but my father, who was a little hard of hearing, strode ahead without apparently noticing the group. We had almost passed them and I was about to heave a huge sigh of relief, when I heard the rasping voice of Bunts addressing his mates again:

'Ah dinna think puir Blondie's quite herself tonight; ah kenned that she could swallow a pint or twa wi' the best o' the lads, but ah warned her the harrd stoff would'na do her nae guid!'

A muffled explosion escaped from my mother, and I had a harder job trying to prove to her that strong liquor was not my métier or even of the slightest interest to me, than I had ever experienced in concealing the truth from her on previous occasions. I saw the light of battle come into her eyes as she considered the possibilities of having me prematurely removed from the WRNS now that the war was nearly over; and I determined to seek my revenge on Bunts at an early opportunity!

By the end of October the Allied forces had advanced across much of northern France and Belgium, and on the night of November 1st a number of our ships took part in the landings at Westkapelle on Walcheren Island. Under cover of fire from the monitor HMS *Erebus* and a small fleet of rocket-ships, the Royal Marine Commandos gained a foothold in Holland and the following day the town of Flushing fell to the British Commander. But this was no easy and comparatively straightforward landing, but a long and arduous battle amongst the sand dunes in which we sustained very heavy losses. Many of our ships never returned from Walcheren Island and the wrecks may still be seen to this day at low water in the estuary of the West Schelde.

The weather was beginning to turn very cold in Southampton, and when my father sent me a fur-lined sleeping-bag for my nineteenth birthday I was at last warm enough to be able to sleep during our nights on duty in the band-room.

Lofty came back in his tank landing-craft late that autumn, for the first time since D-Day, and we had one or two splendid evenings dancing at the Guildhall together. He never referred to his real name or his home county again, and I had learned by then to observe a tactful reticence on the subject.

About this time Eric Wells, Maureen's husband, was given a job at the Air Ministry in London and she began to make inquiries about getting an early discharge from the WRNS.

Perhaps the most exciting event in our lives in November was an examination to become Leading Stokers for which all the Wren Stokers entered at HMS *Squid*. The oral and written parts we passed without much difficulty, but a week or so later I was in the middle of doing the practical side of my exam when an incident occurred which I thought at the time had ruined my chances. I was out in the Cutter 08 near the entrance to the Ocean Dock, with Lt Sherwood acting as coxswain and an Engineer Commander asking me some very searching questions about what I should do with a cracked piston in an emergency. All at once an Aldis lamp began to flash at us from the bridge of a tank landing-craft coming in from seawards, and Lt Sherwood produced a notebook and pencil from his pocket and ordered me to sing out the letters of the message whilst he wrote it down. As the other vessel approached, a figure waving semaphore flags was silhouetted against the sky and I spelt out the letters one by one... LCT 960 to HM TIDDLEY TROT BOAT 08... BUNTS DESIRES MEET STOKES BLUE BOAR 2100 HOURS.

The Engineer Commander was busily engaged tinkering with the engine and I gazed in horror at Lt Sherwood, whilst a cold clammy feeling ran up and down my spine. His face was a mask of complete detachment and immobility, but as I watched him an eyelid solemnly descended to obscure his right eye for a fraction of a second; he closed the notebook and replaced it in his pocket, at the same time murmuring for the benefit of the other officer, 'We'll send this through to HQ as soon as we reach Town Quay.'

A few days later I learnt that I had passed all my exams and could now put a star above the propeller on my right arm, and in due course would be able to wear the much coveted anchor on my left arm.

About this time there was an inter-services chess tournament held in the NAAFI club, for which I decided to enter. After one fairly easy victory I found myself playing against a RAMC Sergeant in the second round. He was an immense hairy gorilla of a man, with small green eyes and a luxuriant black moustache which twitched with nervous excitement when he was considering his next move. Our game lasted for over two hours, until there were only our two kings and two pawns belonging to the Sergeant left on the board. Once his victory was assured, he bared a set of dazzlingly white teeth at me and invited me to join him in a little light refreshment!

By mid-December an easterly gale was blowing, combined with torrential rain and a cold swirling fog. After a few days of unutterable beastliness afloat, I lost my voice completely and started running a temperature; I was put into sick-bay to recover. Three days before Christmas I was back at work again, only to find that our cutter had developed a serious leak and an hourly spell at the pump was hardly enough to keep the water down below the deck-boards. At 5 am the following morning we put her on the slips and in a matter of a few hours we had discovered the leak, recaulked some of the planks and put a patch over the affected area. By Christmas Eve the Cutter o8 was back at work again.

Christmas Day, 1944, dawned in the idyllic sort of way one always dreams of. Overnight a glistening white frost had settled on the Royal Pier like a heavenly benediction, and a midnight-blue sky was gently merging with the first pure pink whisper of dawn on the eastern horizon as we tramped along past the docks on our return from an early service at the Seaman's Mission. Breakfast included such treats as real eggs and the time for a second cup of tea, during which we opened some of our presents; amongst mine was a small compass and a nest of spanners from my father which I exhibited with enormous pride to any receptive audiences.

After breakfast we struggled for some long while to release our boat as the mooring-lines had frozen into stiff hard strips of iron. Underfoot the snow and ice crunched emphatically, and there was no question of running nimbly across the thwarts and along the gunwales. Winkle, Sue and I were dressed in Balaclava helmets, four layers of jerseys and two of trousers, duffel-coats, three layers of socks, sea-boots and minesweeping gloves, and we moved with about as much elasticity as pre-historic mammals traversing hummocks of ice.

Despite the cold it was a gay and cheerful morning with sailors singing Christmas carols on every trip and 'sippers' of rum being offered alongside each ship. We finished work at midday, when the whole of the Starboard Watch had been invited to lunch on the messdeck of LCH 187. A warm and festive atmosphere engulfed us as we descended the long iron ladder in our sea-going apparel; there was holly and mistletoe and multi-coloured balloons festooned around the bulkheads, and our hosts were so anxious to see that we were not under-nourished that I broke the record by having five helpings of turkey followed by three of Christmas pudding, against all my better judgement!

In the evening there was a dance given by HMS *Squid*, with a Royal Marine band which played a rousing selection of Viennese waltzes, tangos, rumbas, polkas and Scottish reels. We had recovered from our Christmas luncheon by then, and we danced and sang until the early hours of December 26th in the warm security of the Royal Hotel, whilst overhead a lone doodle-bug sailed through the starry midnight sky, bound for some unknown destination farther north.

After Christmas the fog returned, followed by a blinding snowstorm. In these polar conditions we groped our way up and down the River Test and Southampton Water, our reds-rimmed eyes peering anxiously into the impenetrable murk. All around us were clusters of white phantom ships, the song of their anchor bells mingling in a weird and muted chorus; even the sailors spoke in muffled whispers, as if the snow had cast a magic spell over the whole vast uproarious universe.

Margaret came over from *Abatos* on New Year's Eve and we went together to a splendid concert and singsong in the NAAFI Club. There must have been nearly a thousand boys and girls there that evening, all singing their hearts out in the poignant knowledge that many of them might be back in Civvy Street by the end of the following year. We sang all the old favourites... 'Lily of Laguna', 'Annie Laurie', 'Pack up your Troubles', 'Every nice Girl loves a Sailor', 'Daisy Bell', 'Shenandoah' and many more besides; and at midnight we joined hands in one gigantic chain to sing 'Auld Lang Syne', and suddenly it all seemed inexpressibly sad to me and I wanted to creep into a hole by myself and cry.

January 1945

Maggie in the stern of the Captain's launch at
Abatos, on a trip up Southampton Water.

HLs *Sea-Mouse* and *Sea-Gull* covered in snow.

February 1945

Margaret, Jilly and Gwen.

Margaret and 3 of the crew of LCH 187.

Bruce and Mary coming out of Beaulieu Abbey with
the Starboard Watch on the left hand side and some
of the crew of LCH 187 on the right hand side.

May 1945

LCT 960 (looking along the tank-deck), covered in flags on VE day.

The crew of the 17 (Diesel Launch). Left to Right:

Back row: Peter MacDonald, Joel Perkins (Coxswain).

Front row: Robert Lobden (Wee Jock), Archibald Johnston (Stox).

Tony and Di on board LCT 532.

July 1945

The Starboard Watch on the Royal Pier. Left to Right:

Back row: Sylvia Sunderland, Gina Ritchie,
Heather Cotton, Diana Bane, Me, 'Tommy' Hill.

Middle row: Gwen Bagg, Betty Altwood (Attwood?),
'Winkle' Preece, Sue (D'wash?), Eve Sugg, Dottie Brown.

Front row: Margaret Sparkes, Gilly Sparkes,
Lt Sherwood, PO Gwen Dobson, Joan Horton.

September 1945

Gay Marshall outside Tideways.

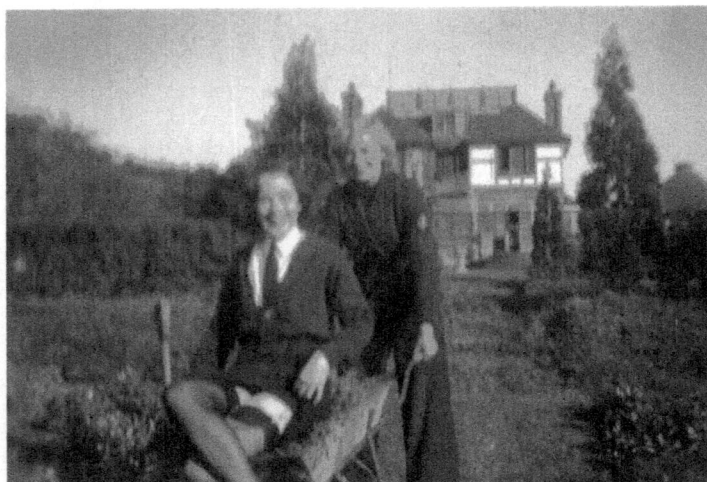

Me wheeling Gay in a wheelbarrow in Tideways garden.

October 1945

Alanna's stern and the MN Training Yacht *Moyana*.

November 1945

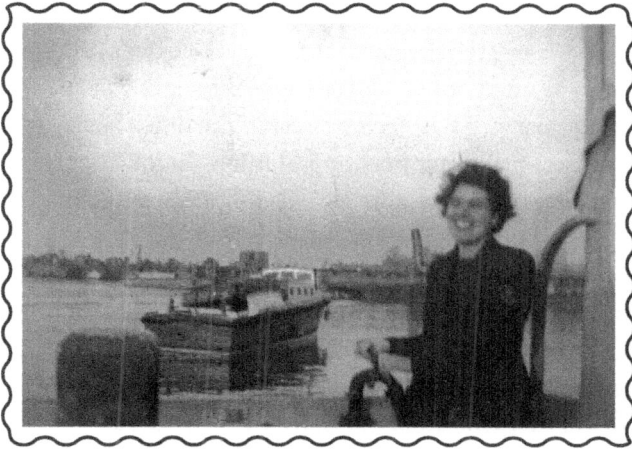

Bee, pumping out the *Sea-Cow's* bilges, with the crash-boat astern.

9

The Year of the Victories

THE ARCTIC WEATHER continued through most of January, and by the end of the month we had become well acclimatized to the snow and ice. Our trips to and fro amongst the landing-craft were enlivened by a great deal of snowballing, and when we were off duty Winkle, Sue and I sometimes took three toboggans across on the ferry to Hythe and raced each other down the hills amongst the pine woods.

Apart from the old charcoal stove, there was no other form of heating in the band-room and there came a time towards the end of the month when all the pipes froze on the outside of the building and we could no longer get any water to flow from the taps. This presented a serious problem, both for cooking and washing, until Tarzan appeared one evening with a wheelbarrow which he told us he had borrowed from a garden in Shirley; he filled it with blocks of frozen snow from the pier, which we then melted in saucepans over the stove. All this took a long time and, to add to our troubles, there were severe gales blowing for days on end and our boat began to suffer from recurrent engine trouble, so that she was often out of commission. Whenever this happened we used to volunteer to go as crew on one of the other boats, as many of the girls did not really enjoy boating in mid-winter.

The air-raid warnings seldom sounded in those days, but there were many nights when doodle-bugs sailed across the dark sky above us, intent on their mission of death and destruction somewhere away to the north. That winter seemed to be full of hard frosty moonlit nights, with icy waves breaking over the bows and strange bodies moving silently amongst the stars.

Early in February the big thaw set in, and the Cutter 08 continued to break down at the most inconvenient moments. Her engine was long overdue for a thorough overhaul as it had been running continuously for nearly ten months. Winkle and I developed streaming colds in sympathy with the thaw and the engine, and the days passed in gloomy anticipation of the immediate future.

About this time we spent many of our evenings off duty at the NAAFI Club, where there were concerts, dances, ping-pong tournaments and plenty of cheerful company to dispel our fits of depression. Already we had started wondering about what we should do when no more girls were needed to work on boats, at the end of the war. The idea of settling down on land again did not appeal to either of us, and one day we took our courage in both hands and called at some of the Merchant Navy shipping offices in Southampton to see if we could sign on as stewardesses on one of the big liners. Everywhere we received discouraging replies; the jobs were so sought after that the companies refused to employ anyone who was not a relative of a man serving in that line; also they indicated that we should do better to wait another ten years before applying for such a job. Our future began to look very dark indeed.

At the end of February my mother and father came south again, to spend a long week-end at Winchester. Sue and I hitch-hiked over there on the Saturday afternoon, and for the last part of the journey we were offered a lift on a horse-drawn vehicle carrying a tall load of hay on the very pinnacle of which we perched ourselves happily.

Later that evening Sue brought her mother to dine with us at the Royal Hotel where my parents were staying. After a pleasant enough dinner we moved into the lounge, and I remember straining my ears to overhear a conversation between my mother and Mrs Huish, who were seated side by side on the sofa. The gist of it ran as follows:

My mother—'I hope this wretched war will soon be over so that I can get the child back home again.'

Sue's mother—'I think my Sue will be quite sorry to leave the WRNS, she does so love being on a boat.'

My mother—'I know, but the poor children don't know what they're missing; all this terrible hard work and no chance to enjoy themselves and meet any really nice young men. And one doesn't know what sort of people they have to mix with.'

Sue's mother (well aware that I was listening, although appearing to be deep in conversation with Sue and my father)—'I am trying to arrange for Sue to take a course at the Cordon Bleu when she gets demobbed, as I don't think she'll be very happy sitting at home doing nothing for long.'

My mother—'I intend to see that my child does not get entangled in some silly job as she threatened my husband the other day. Of course she must have a coming-out dance, and I want her to go to Queen Charlotte's Ball and do a season in London, and enjoy going to all the parties and dances we can arrange for her.'

At this point a sickly and unpleasant expression must have appeared on my face, for my father asked me what was the matter and had I, perhaps, eaten something for dinner which had disagreed with me?

Next morning we went to a beautiful service in Winchester Cathedral and then to visit my father's old college and the house in which he lived as a schoolboy. That same evening Sue and I were back at work on our boat, ferrying a full load of lustily singing drunks from Town Quay out to the *Empire Dockland* on A Trot. My mother's conversation the previous night and the words of 'Maggie May' seemed to be chasing each other round and round inside my brain, and all sorts of complicated questions erupted from this whirlpool. I knew that it would be unbearable to lead a life of luxury and idleness after the last two years, but how could I get my parents to under-stand? I had found many of the answers to my problems in the writings of Tolstoy, especially a remarkable book of his called *Resurrection*, but how could I explain all these terribly important things at home, when I usually became inarticulate and tongue-tied as soon as I opened my mouth?

Early in March, Mary Pocock, one of the coxswains on the Starboard Watch, was married to the skipper of LCH 187, the ship in which we had been invited to luncheon on Christmas Day. The wedding took place at Beaulieu Abbey and we were all there to act as Mary's guard of honour. When the couple emerged from the church at the end of the service, they walked down a long avenue of sailors and Boats' Crew Wrens, under an archway of crossed boat-hooks held above them. It was a splendid sight in the early spring sunshine, with a symphony of blackbirds and thrushes singing in the trees around the abbey.

On March 24th the Allied forces crossed the Rhine in three places, and the victory in Europe seemed very close indeed. A new order was issued at HMS *Squid*, to the effect that we could now go ashore in civilian clothes when off duty. Winkle, Sue and I emerged one spring evening, clad in extraordinary pre-war garments which we filled like a trio of well-stuffed sofas. We had certain misgivings about our appearance, as to whether it really represented the height of fashion in 1945, but, nevertheless, we ventured forth to a dance at the Guildhall and put on a bold front to carry us through the ordeal. Gum-chewing Yanks wandered up and said 'Hi, Baby!' as they pinched us speculatively, and I was about to beat a hasty retreat when I caught the eye of Lofty, whose normally placid expression was transformed into a look of utter astonishment. Once the initial shock was over we danced happily the whole evening, and I found myself wondering what the deb dances would be like and whether I should ever find any partners who danced as well as Lofty in the days to come.

Easter Sunday was on April 1st, and it was a day of brilliant sunshine, gale force winds and much song and laughter. Gone was the tension of a year ago, when the troops were busy training for the Second Front and no one dared think of the future; now that the end was so nearly in sight, everyone was talking about good old Civvy Street and the marvellous things that lay in store for them and what you could do with their old winkle-barges, as the landing-craft were called, once they'd got their perishing tickets.

Later on that month LCT 960 went to Walcheren Island and Zuid Beveland on a short mission, and Bunts returned from there with a present for me in the shape of a pair of wooden sabots.

'Ah dinna ken if they'll fit you, forbye,' he announced anxiously. 'But ah took the measure o' yon sea-boots juist before we were awa' to Holland.'

My sea-boots were size 8, three sizes bigger than I normally take, so I had no difficulty in slipping on the Dutch sabots and assuring Bunts that they felt as comfortable and commodious as bedroom slippers!

'Och, ay! They look grand!' beamed the proud signalman. 'Will ye nae wear them tonight, and join the lads for a wee dram at the Dancing Bear?'

On May 2nd the German forces in Italy and part of Austria surrendered to General Alexander, and the following day the Russians marched into Berlin. Two days later all the German forces in North Germany, Holland and Denmark surrendered to Montgomery, and May 8th was a day of great rejoicing, VE Day, when the Allies celebrated their ultimate victory in Europe.

All the ships on Southampton Water were arrayed in flags and rainbow-coloured bunting, and their fog-horns and sirens blared incessantly, from dawn until long after midnight. By mid-morning most of the sailors were drunk and we had a hectic time delivering them to the right ships, dodging fireworks and rockets which seemed to come at us from all directions, refusing innumerable 'gulpers' of rum and avoiding the American liberty-boats which were roaring up and down Southampton Water on zig-zag courses, utterly oblivious to the Rule of the Road.

I was off duty that evening, and long before darkness fell there were bonfires alight all over the town and hundreds of people dancing round them with a gay abandon which they had not felt for many a day. Up and down the main street gangs of soldiers, sailors and civilians who had never met before in their lives, marched arm in arm, twenty or so abreast, singing lustily as they swung their arms and legs in a bold rhythm. A group of stout matrons advanced like a platoon of tanks towards the Bar Gate, exchanging bawdy jokes and sharp repartee with the crowds who impeded their progress. One of them wore a tall straw hat with the legend 'Kiss me Quick' embroidered round the brim, a souvenir from a brewery outing one summer before the war.

In the midst of all this happy turmoil I was beginning to feel rather lost and bewildered, when suddenly, like the sun emerging from behind a bank of dark clouds, I saw the crew of LCT 1109 crossing the road towards me. Most of them came from the north country, Yorkshire, Lancashire and Cheshire, and we had long since established a firm bond of friendship because I was born in Yorkshire too; without a doubt 1109 was my favourite landing-craft on all the trots in Southampton Water, and it seemed like the kindly hand of fate which had arranged for this chance encounter on VE Night. From then onwards I began to enjoy myself as much as anyone else in England that evening.

The skipper led the way into the Red Lion but Wee Jock, a very small seaman not much above five feet high, was first at the bar to order a round of black and tans.

'Drink oop, lass!' advised the coxswain, who had just given a spirited rendering of 'On Ilkla Moor Baht 'At' with his mouth-organ. 'T'night is summat out o' the ornnery rocn o' things an' ye'll have to hoorry oop te keep abreast o' the lads!'

Leading Seaman Jim Dawson was a teetotaller himself, but he was not averse to the lads having a drink, especially if there was a bit of music to help it on its way. I never heard another man who could play such a lively and captivating tune on the mouth-organ, and when he and Joe, the seaman from Lancashire, played a duet and all the lads began to sing, as likely as not a few old ladies in the pub would start sobbing into their pints of Guinness before many minutes had passed.

Stripey, the old stoker who had been in the navy since he was a boy, had a faraway look in his eyes after the coxswain and Joe had played 'My Little Grey Home in the West'.

'Ay, that were right champion!' he murmured with deep conviction. 'I nivver thowt te hear sich a grand ole song. By gow! I reckon them lads dorn't knaw that they could be coining brass oop t'big the-aters in Loondon.'

After an hour or so we left the Red Lion and drifted on across the flaming city. Everywhere the long curling tongues of fire rose up to greet the stars from a thousand dancing crackling bonfires, and then the lights came on all over England... At first we did not realize what was happening, so accustomed were we to the blackout, but suddenly the full impact hit us just as a mighty carillon of bells rang out triumphantly from the belfry of St. Michael's Church. I believe it was Ken, the Motor Mechanic, who first suggested going to church; normally a crowd of sailors ashore for an evening's fun would be as unlikely a sight to find inside a church as a cluster of nuns aboard a warship! But there was some special kind of magic in the air on VE Night and the most unusual things were taking place all around us.

St. Michael's was overflowing with servicemen and women, all singing happily, their faces radiant with joy as they thought of their future in the brave new world. After the last hymn we drifted on through the brilliantly illuminated streets until we came to the Guildhall. There was a wild and wonderful dance taking place outside the building, on the concrete terrace, up and down the steps and all over the grass square which formed the heart of Southampton. A powerful band was playing, with numerous loudspeakers relaying the music to all four corners of the earth, and on that one night everyone loved his neighbours and forgave his enemies, and a future of exceeding brightness appeared to face the people of Britain.

Inevitably, a period of anticlimax followed VE Day. The next afternoon a large group of people wearing civilian clothes invaded the sanctity of the Royal Pier and sat around in the sunshine on what we had come to regard as our benches. The moment of goodwill amongst all men had passed, and we gazed at these intruders with hostile stares, hoping to uproot them by the glacierlike quality of our reception.

Afloat, life was much as usual, and there was one memorable afternoon off duty when the skipper of the Hythe Ferry allowed me to steer his vessel from Hythe Pier back to Southampton and to bring her alongside the jetty at the end of the journey.

Some of the landing-craft were drafted away to other ports, and a number of them made preparations for paying off their crews, who were being sent out to the Far East where the war was still raging. One such tank landing-craft had a large mongrel dog aboard, a fine ginger and white beast with the head of an Irish sheepdog and a pair of sad brown eyes which regarded the world with timid apprehension. He had been across to Normandy on D-Day and had lived down in the engine-room when the shelling grew fierce on the beaches; as a result the poor animal had burnt his pads so badly that he could hardly walk, and his fur was in a wretched mangy condition. One of the crew told me that they would have to get him put to sleep before they left Southampton, as they could not take him out east with them.

As soon as I came off duty that afternoon I ran to the nearest post office to wire my mother. I was due for long leave at the end of May and I sent the following telegram home: 'May I bring large mangy dog home on Friday? He took part in invasion of Europe. Love, Rozelle.' I believed that the last piece of information would be the vital factor to sway my parents' judgement and gain their approval of this unusual request. Next morning their reply reached me at breakfast-time: 'Expect you both Friday evening. Love, Mother and Father.'

A few dreadful hours ensued before I could reach the landing-craft with the dog, as I thought they might already have taken him ashore to the vet to be put to sleep. My fears were groundless and a few days later I found myself boarding the train to Waterloo, accompanied by a very large orange and white dog. In due course we reached London, but there was a long wait at King's Cross before my next train left for the north. I had called the dog 'Sailor', and he and I sat in a corner of the buffet having tea. Presently a group of soldiers strolled across and offered my companion a sip of beer which he liked so well that one of them bought him a whole pint. He drank it up like a connoisseur, making appreciative smacking noises with his lips and tongue, and immediately he became the focus of attention in the railway buffet; a dog that could sup his pint like a man!

Some hours later we landed at Retford Station and Sailor wove a zig-zag course across the platform to greet my parents. He was the sort of large and gentle beast that everybody loved, and I knew at once that he would be firmly established in his new home in a couple of hours. Sailor lived with us until he died, some eight or nine years later, and he was the noblest dog we ever had.

During that leave we went to Yorkshire to stay in my grandfather's old house at Keighley, and I spent many hours tramping across the

moors above Wharfedale and Airedale and around Wuthering Heights.
I vividly remember the pleasure of being on those windswept heights
again; the smell of sun-kissed heather and bracken, the long hard lines
made by the black stone walls meandering across the barren countryside
into infinity and the shadows of great cumulus clouds chasing each
other across the purple landscape. This land is far removed from the
soft and rolling English countryside of the south, for it is a hard strong
place where the tall black chimneys smoking away in the valleys seem
to be in harmony with the lonely and desolate moorland above them.
But it is a grand place to live in, and an immense surge of pride swept
over me as I surveyed the West Riding from the top of Morton Moor.

By mid-summer our days in Southampton were numbered. The
22nd Flotilla left there early in July, and hardly a day passed without
some familiar ship disappearing off the trots or some old friend coming
round to say goodbye. It was a sad time in many ways, but there was
one unforgettable day which left a lasting impression on Sue and me. A
certain minesweeper, BYMS 2059, had recently come to Southampton
and been allotted a berth alongside the Royal Pier. It was not long
before we became acquainted with the skipper and crew, and found
ourselves helping to paint the ship's hull on our afternoons off duty.
As a reward for this task, which both of us had enjoyed enormously,
we were invited to spend a whole day aboard our minesweeper doing
speed trials and compass swinging out beyond the Solent. Lt Sherwood
arranged for two stand-ins for us for the afternoon trips, and we headed
out to sea one summer's morning, light-headed with excitement at
finding ourselves on such a large and wonderful vessel. It was a perfect
July day, with fleecy white clouds moving slowly, like grazing flocks of
sheep, across a sky of cornflower blue beneath which lay a sea of purest
jade green, interspersed with a few dazzling white waves. The bows of
the minesweeper rose and fell in a steady rhythm and a rainbow made
of priceless emeralds, sapphires, rubies and topazes formed across our
bow-wave and kept company with us all day long, only changing from
port to starboard now and then, when the ship's course was altered for
the swinging of the compass.

We lolled around in the sunshine like passengers on a cruising liner, climbed the rigging, explored the mysteries of the bridge and engine-room, had lunch and high tea on the mess-deck and made many new friends. When BYMS 2059 was sent to the Far East soon afterwards, we kept in touch with her for many months and the memory of that glorious day will never fade.

On July 26th the results of the General Election were announced, with a resounding swing from Tory to Labour; Clement Attlee replaced Winston Churchill as our Prime Minister.

A few days later all the Boats' Crew Wrens at HMS *Squid* were disbanded and sent on draft. Amidst a whirl of packing and saying goodbye to so many old friends, Winkle and I learnt that Joel Perkins, the coxswain of Diesel Launch 17, had been taken seriously ill, and we went to visit him on our last evening in Southampton. It was raining hard that night and it seemed to us that even the sky was weeping bitter tears because the many happy months which we had spent in that motley seaport had now, irrevocably, drawn to a close.

Already Sue had gone to HMS *Turtle* at Poole, and Winkle and I were amongst the last to leave Southampton on August Ist. We reached the station in a state of utter dejection, to find a large assembly of sailors waiting there, who had come to give us a true naval send-off on our journey to Portsmouth. As the train pulled out of the station and gathered way, I felt a great lump in my throat and I was glad when the wreaths of smoke from the funnel finally obscured the waving, cheering throng.

Winkle and I were sent to the Solent Hotel in Southsea, which was then a branch of the WRNS Drafting Depot, and immediately we stepped back into a half-forgotten world of nearly two years ago. We scrubbed and polished the decks, did squad drill, attended lectures about what to do in Civvy Street, went dancing at Kimballs and South Parade Pier and longed, with a kind of hopeless desperation, to be sent to another base where they still needed Boats' Crew Wrens. We were there for two weeks altogether, and undoubtedly the most stirring event during that period was attending Divisions one morning at HMS *Excellent*. About forty Wrens and five hundred gunnery officers and ratings took part in the parade, and we all marched round the gigantic parade ground in the middle of Whale Island, to the magnificent music of the Royal Marine Band. Then followed a short service and an address given by the Commodore, after which each squad in turn marched past the dais on which stood the Senior Officers, and the Commodore instructed a Petty Officer to write on a slate his impressions of the squad which had just passed; a rating was then dispatched at the double, to run to the front of the squad and hold up the slate, so that everyone could see how they had fared in the parade. All this time the band was playing, and many of the officers and men were carrying swords or bayonets. It was a grand sight and one which I would have been sorry to miss.

Soon after our arrival at the Drafting Depot, Lt Sherwood made a special journey to Portsmouth to see the Chief Wren Officer on our behalf, and as a result of his kind intervention, Winkle and I found our names up on the drafting board to go to HMS *Tormentor* on August 15th. It so happened that it was VJ Day, when the victory against Japan was finally declared. All the ships' sirens started blaring again and we travelled through a maze of celebrations, bonfires and fireworks, but we took no part in the festivities on this occasion for both of us felt vaguely unhappy at the imminent approach of our demob dates.

Tormentor had changed very little since the time I left there in the spring of 1944, but the general outlook on life had altered completely. Instead of the tension and uncertainty about the future which was common before D-Day, everyone now seemed to be looking ahead towards some glossy dream world which went under the heading of Civvy Street. Every day the navy was contracting and withdrawing into a remote and exclusively small circle. The Hamble flowed up and down, oblivious to the affairs of men, and some of the bigger yachts appeared, mysteriously, overnight and crept back on to their accustomed moorings along the tortuous river.

Winkle and I went to live in Sunburst, the last house in the country lane which ran along the crest of the hills above Warsash. To begin with there was very little work for us to do and we spent our time cleaning and doing a number of repairs on the few remaining Wrens' boats, in the hopes of being invited to act as their crew.

My parents came to stay on the Isle of Wight for a short holiday and I was allowed a great deal of free time to visit them. After a week or so Winkle went away to Havant on an agricultural course, and I found myself acting as stoker on the crash-boat, a fast twin-engined launch which was mainly used by the Commander of the base. Commander MacBrayne, RN, was a man who took a personal interest in everyone under his command, and at church parade on a Sunday he was able to remember the smallest details about the private lives and worries or joys of any rating he might care to speak to. He was the complete father to the huge motley family who were spending their last days in the navy at HMS *Tormentor*, and I never met another skipper who was more devoted to his crew.

We made a number of voyages to the Isle of Wight and Netley and the Beaulieu River, sometimes with the Commander's wife and a couple of other naval officers and their wives and dogs aboard. It was all very relaxed and friendly, and I was beginning to enjoy myself on the crash-boat when I was suddenly transferred to a long sleek-hulled boat called *Alanna*, whose coxswain was the famous Jimmy Edwards, the terror of *Tormentor*.

Before very long I found myself working tremendously hard again, helping Jimmy to tow groups of small landing-craft to their appointed berths up and down the river. She was the hardest taskmaster I had ever encountered, but she was also the true perfectionist on a boat and she taught me more in a few days than I had learnt in my previous two years in the WRNS. Jimmy Edwards was still wearing one of the First World War type of Wren's hat, and, contrary to all regulations, her white bitch, Sue-Dog, accompanied us on all our trips. After a few gruelling days in which I began to learn the theory of towing all shapes and sizes of vessels in all conditions of weather, Jimmy allowed me to steer *Alanna* and then to take an LCP(L) out entirely alone and tow another similar boat back to the pool at *Tormentor*. Suddenly I began to perceive that towing was a very skilful and specialized task, and although the skin on my hands was torn to ribbons with so much handling of wet ropes, I felt that I was doing the most thrilling job in the whole of the British Navy!

As the autumn advanced and grey fogs began to enshroud the river at dawn, Jimmy and I used to take a boat each out to the Hamble Point Buoy around 6.30 am, and drop anchor there to wait for tank landing-craft searching for the river entrance on the rising tide. Some mornings it was indescribably lovely out there in our remote world of grey and pink vapours, with a sea made of shimmering moonstones and a few small birds crying plaintively on the mud-banks near at hand. Then there would be the thumping of ship's propellers and the distant muttering of powerful engines, and suddenly our phantom vessels would arise cautiously out of the mist. Those landing-craft that came with the October dawns were nearly always new to the river, and we would each put a line on to the vessel of our choice and tow them into the river and up to their appointed berths. Occasionally one of my favourite ships from Southampton appeared at the rendezvous, and then there would be mugs of tea strongly laced with rum passed across before the towing-line had a chance to become taut.

All through October we went on towing ships to their mud-berths, winter-berths, peacetime-berths and various other berths, and thanks to Jimmy Edwards I grew more and more confident as the days grew shorter. On October 23rd we towed the beautiful training yacht *Moyana* off a sand-bank where she had run aground, and the same afternoon I was sent up to the base to see the First Officer who told me that my hook had come through and I was now a Leading Wren.

About this time Winkle was drafted away to another base, and I spent my time off duty going to visit old friends. Maureen had been demobbed by then and she and Eric were living in a flat in London whilst he worked at the Air Ministry. One afternoon I spent at their home and the three of us went to the ballet at Sadler's Wells that evening, a new and very enjoyable experience for me.

On another occasion I hitch-hiked to Poole to visit Sue and spent the night in a long Nissen hut on the edge of the harbour, which was the

Boats' Crew Wrens quarters at HMS *Turtle*. Some of our old cutters from Southampton had been brought to Poole, and many of the landing-craft were there too. In the morning we did several trips around the trots which were filled with nostalgic encounters; and we also found time to land on a small island clad in heather and dwarf pine trees, a sort of Robinson Crusoe island which we explored with the same childish delight as if it had been a desert island located in mid-Atlantic.

Towards the end of October I was sitting on the top of a bus going into Portsmouth one afternoon, when a red-headed sailor with an attractive smile came and sat down beside me. He was a wireman called Don from LCT 576, and he came originally from Stepney. Before we had reached Fareham, Don revealed to me that he used to be a real skunk and a rotter, but he had recently been converted and was now on the straight and narrow and no mistake! A few minutes later he invited me home for tea which I thought was rather sudden, but imagined the invitation was not fraught with any unforeseen dangers if the man was really telling the truth about being such a reformed character. Anyhow, I accepted, and in due course we arrived at the home of a Mr and Mrs Thomson in Rubin Road, Northend, which I afterwards came to know as 'No. 20 Mess'. There were several other Wrens and sailors already there when Don and I arrived, and everyone seemed very friendly and cheerful in a determined sort of way. The Thomsons had two small boys who were told to bring in the tea, and we were soon seated around a large oval table, helping ourselves to spam sandwiches and home-made Madeira cake. There was quite a spread and I was beginning to feel warm and mellow with a coal fire crackling in the hearth just behind me, when suddenly Mr Thomson got up and announced that we would now sing a few hymns; he bawled the opening bars of 'Lead us, heavenly Father, lead us', at the same time conducting with a dessert-spoon which he brandished above the teapot in a forceful manner. You could have knocked me down with a feather, as the saying goes!

It appeared that No. 20 Mess was called 'home' by a number of sailors, Wrens and civilians, who had all been 'converted' by the Thomsons, themselves fanatically ardent Baptists. One had to confess all one's sins publicly at a service in the hideous Baptist chapel, after which one could get re-baptized on the beach in Southsea and start life again as a new person, having cast off all the wicked and sinful traits of one's youth. I did not feel inclined to take the plunge right away, so I played along with the members of No. 20 Mess for some while, trying to decide what I felt about them. Prayers and hymns in the middle of masticating Grade III salmon sandwiches struck me as being ostentatious and even blasphemous, and I felt very embarrassed one evening when we all sallied forth behind Mr Thomson and marched up and down the main street in Northend, accosting people waiting in cinema queues or outside pubs to tell them that their ways were evil and would lead to eternal damnation, and they had far better come home with us!

For some weeks I wavered on the brink as I was fairly susceptible to new ideas at the age of nineteen, and a girl called Lea had told me how gloriously released and happy she felt since her conversion. She did not entirely convince me, and anyway I felt serenely happy when I was working on a boat and had no desire to be released from that sort of life.

The end came quite suddenly, in the middle of a southerly gale . Jimmy had gone to London for the day, and that morning the flood tide came roaring into the River Hamble with the pent-up fury of a bursting dam. I was in sole charge of *Alanna*, with a busy day of towing, fetching and carrying ahead of me. Icy pellets of driving rain beat into my face and the wind howled dismally in the bare trees along the river banks; and suddenly I knew, with a blinding flash of insight, that it would be hypocritical to go on pretending that the Thomsons' set-up was the right life for me. I felt exhilarated by the stormy weather and somehow cleansed from the extraordinary experience which had threatened to engulf me.

The autumn days were drawing in, and even the indefatigable Jimmy began to realize that our towing jobs would soon be growing few and far between. The sense of urgency with which all her work had been inspired during the past five years imperceptibly grew less, and now and then we had time to brew a pot of tea on the primus stove aboard *Alanna* and Jimmy would talk about her great dream for the future... To run a boatbuilding yard of her own on the west coast of Scotland.

My mother was becoming restive at home because many of my friends had already been demobbed, and she had heard some alarming rumours about minefields along the South Coast. Unbeknown to me, she must have written a tiresome letter to the Commander, because my father showed me his reply next time I went home on leave...

> HMS *Tormentor*,
> Warsash, Hants.
> 31st October, 1945.

Dear Madam,

In reply to your letter of Saturday last, I can assure you that your daughter is safe from floating mines, it being our policy to refrain from sending any boats into dangerous areas.

Your daughter is well looked after and happy, and you can rest assured that she will not be sent into any danger.

> Yours sincerely,
> AB MacBrayne
> Commander, RN
> Commanding Officer

Soon after this my mother heard another rumour to the effect that one was allowed fifty-six days demob leave, after which the Labour Exchange would uproot one from a life of leisure and direct one into a suitable job. I was delighted when the rumour reached my ears, but my mother was furious and we had a long and exhausting tussle on this thorny subject, each of us determined only to see one side of the question.

On November 1st we had real eggs for supper at Sunburst, perhaps to compensate for losing *Alanna*. One day she was there, lying peacefully alongside the Rising Sun Pier, and the next morning she had gone. Perhaps her pre-war owners had come to claim her; I never did discover what became of her, but we mourned her departure bitterly, especially as there was only one boat, the *Sea-Cow*, left for the Wrens to run.

November drifted quietly by. There was very little work for us to do and most of the time a girl called Bee Doyle and I sat around on the *Sea-Cow* waiting for signals to get under way, and often waiting in vain. Bee came from Eltham in south-east London, and we had many long and earnest discussions about our future lives.

I went home for my twentieth birthday, my last leave before being demobbed. It was filled with luncheon and dinner parties, thé dansants and cocktail dansants; everyone celebrating the end of the war and making gay plans for the future. I must have been poor company amongst that cheerful throng, already indulging in their new-found peacetime complacency.

The day after I returned from leave, Bee and I had the unhappy task of handing over the *Sea-Cow* to her new crew of sailors. The category of Boats' Crew Wrens had come to an abrupt end and the men were taking over the Wrens' boats at every base in the British Isles. It was indeed a sad moment.

On November 28th I started work in the Information Office at *Tormentor*, as the Education Officer's secretary. I sat at my desk behind a large typewriter every day, doing very little very slowly indeed. By the end of the first week I could type one whole page of foolscap in four hours, and I had become quite an authority on what to do in Civvy Street. Each morning a group of sailors would come to our office to get information, and when the Education Officer was out I had to improvise for him. A typical conversation went as follows...

'Mornin', Stokes. Where's the geezer wot runs this orfice?'

'He's gone across to Hamble to get some more books, Nobby.'

'Well you'll 'ave te do instead! Wot ah wants te know is, 'ow do ah git into this 'ere boatbuilding lark darn sarth? It suits me 'ealth darn 'ere, see, an' you can keep the Big Smoke as fer as ah'm concerned.'

'Oh, I can tell you all about jobs in the boat-building firms round these parts, because that's just the sort of lark I'm interested in myself!'

'Ah allus told ma mates you was some perishin' use te the King's navy, Blondie! Just you 'and over the dope, an' the best o' British luck te you!'

The next man in the queue would probably fancy himself as a butcher, and the one after said he was looking for a nice cosy billet where he could sit on his arse all day long doing damn all; he thought perhaps a library or a job in the GPO would suit him.

None of us knew much about the possibilities for employment after the war, but a great pile of pamphlets arrived on government grants, technical courses and evening classes, and the men who were waiting so impatiently for their demobs. foresaw nothing but a future of golden opportunities. The exceptions were those whose wives or fiancées had eloped with Yanks or whose prospects at home were so gloomy that they determined to sign on for seven years in the navy, a bold decision which few of their mates could understand.

By the beginning of December Sue had already been demobbed and Winkle was back at the Drafting Depot in Portsmouth. They both came over to Warsash one week-end to have a farewell re-union with me. After a busy morning scrubbing and polishing the cabin for Captain's rounds, we took the bus into Southampton and found our beloved cutter, 08, waiting to go on a trip from Town Quay. Her new men's crew allowed us to take over for an hour or so, and we had a grand time visiting the last of the landing-craft on 2 and 3 Trots.

Later on that evening we went to a dance at the NAAFI Club, and returned to Warsash in time to check in at 10 pm. Then we climbed out through one of the rear windows of Sunburst and sat on the shingle beach below the house for a long while, talking about all the most important things in our little world and listening to the sad song of the winter sea, sighing as it kissed the fat round pebbles along the foreshore.

Gradually the days drew in and the cold grey mantle of winter descended upon the naval base. Each week a few more people packed their bags and left for Civvy Street, and those who were left behind moved slower and slower, like clockwork mice which are only waiting to be rewound.

On December 19th we had our Christmas dance at Hamblemeads, the principal Wren's quarters at *Tormentor*. There was a large and beautiful Christmas tree with a silver angel playing a violin on the topmost branch, and there were Chinese lanterns and multi-coloured balloons and splendid food and drink which tasted like nectar fit for the Gods. The moon shone serenely over the River Hamble that night, and the stars twinkled merrily down on a boatload of Christmas carollers singing 'Holy Night' as they chugged along the river. Up at Hamblemeads the dance band played all the old familiar tunes and for the last time there was one big family at HMS *Tormentor*, dancing and singing together as if it was the last dance in creation.

The next two days had a nightmare quality about them. I spring-cleaned the Information Office, had a demob medical inspection, went to my last pay-muster, then did demobbing rounds. I said goodbye to all my friends, packed my belongings and took my bicycle to the station to be sent home by rail.

On the morning of December 22nd all the formalities had been completed and I was ready to go. Just before midday I was ushered into the Commander's office to say goodbye and receive a few words of advice on how to comport myself in civilian life. He started by telling me that I had been a reasonably good stoker, or words to that effect, and the navy would be sorry to lose me but that Civvy Street had considerable advantages to offer and he knew for a certainty that my parents would be very glad to have me back.

I had managed to get through the previous two days in a numbed sort of misery, but suddenly I felt I could bear it no longer. When the Commander murmured something about making himself personally responsible for seeing that I was offered an interesting job in a boatbuilding firm, I suddenly lost all control, and bursting into floods of tears ran blindly from his office into the brave new world outside.

Rising Sun Pier and Jetty at sunset.

The tow path and River Hamble.

The Engineering Yard.

LCPL188 under way, with Fairey's Aviation Works behind.

Epilogue

I T IS NOW twenty-five years, or a quarter of a century, since the end of the Second World War, and the brave new world which I ventured into with such misgivings on the day I left the WRNS has matured into a world of scientific progress, changing values and new 'scenes', precariously clinging to the solid structure of an old civilization, like a fast-growing ivy covering the mellow pink bricks of a Georgian house.

Many people of middle-age and over are apt to drone like a swarm of bees about the good old days and the evils of the present generation; as if there had not always been good old days for thousands of years, and bad ones too, which are never mentioned on these occasions. Nothing really changes in the everlasting cycle of existence; each age brings forth its heroes and its cowards, its wise men and its fools, but they wear a different garb which sometimes makes them hard to recognize.

In the past year or so a few heroic men have pioneered a pathway to the moon and other men, entirely alone, have circumnavigated our world non-stop in a small sailing-vessel. Simultaneously large groups of long-haired bums have marched on London Town in the cause of peace, and beaten up unarmed policemen to emphasize their noble aims. Which all goes to prove that the world of today is just as full of contrasts as it was in the long dark years of 1939-45.

The five girls, Maureen, Margaret, Anne, Sue and Winkle, who became my greatest friends during the months we spent together in the WRNS, have remained so ever since. Some of us are still able to meet at regular intervals, whilst the others who live too far away fill the gap with a steady correspondence which does much to maintain the friendship we valued so highly in those wartime days.

The lives of those five girls, three of them stokers and the other two deck-hands in the Royal Navy, have developed along such widely different lines that they might be likened to a five-pointed star, leading the eye towards five remote points on the celestial compass.

Maureen, who was the first to leave the WRNS, was married to Eric during the summer of 1945. They lived in London. whilst he was working at the Air Ministry, and then in Cornwall for a short while, and it was there that Maureen's first child, Treve, was born.

Eric became the Managing Director of the Australian subsidiary of a well-known Cornish firm who manufactured air compressors and other pneumatic equipment, and when he and his family returned to Australia, he spent the next twenty years building a branch of this firm there which was to become a proud limb of its parent. During those years the Wells family lived in Melbourne and Maureen had three other children, all of them girls. Treve and his three sisters have all won scholarships to universities, one of them to the USA, and Treve is now working in England, the land of his birth, as an economist statistician in a semi-government concern dealing with home-grown cereals.

Most of Maureen's life has been spent as a housewife, mother, gardener and help to Eric in his business. but she has also developed her talent as a free-lance writer, and she has had numerous poems and articles published in Australian magazines. and newspapers.

When Margaret left the WRNS, she went back to Oxford for a year to get her Diploma in Education, and then she took her first teaching job, from 1947-50, at Cheltenham Ladies' College.

By then her parents were getting elderly and rather frail, so she decided to move to her home-town of Exeter in order to be near them. She started teaching in a private school, St. Margaret's School, in Exeter, and when the Headmistress, who owned the school, retired some two years later, Margaret was invited to succeed her. The school then became a charitable company, its only income being from fees. Margaret remained there as Headmistress for eight years, virtually working herself to a standstill, as she had to combine a heavy teaching programme with being Housemistress of the boarders, and acting as her own secretary as well.

At the end of that period she was very tired indeed, her parents had died and she felt it was time she had a change, so she went as the Head of Classics to Kenya High School in Nairobi. It was a European school which was just opening up to Africans and Asians, so Margaret arrived there at a crucial moment and spent four exceedingly interesting years in East Africa. During her holidays she managed to travel as much as possible to various Game Parks, the Victoria Falls, much of South Africa, and even on a safari to the summit of Kilimanjaro (19,000 feet). Her journey back to England was not uneventful either; she travelled by taxi to Juba in southern Sudan, flew on to Khartoum and then crossed the desert by train to Wadi Halfa. There were no other Europeans on this part of the journey. Margaret then boarded a steamer to Aswan, stopping en route to see the temple at Abu Simbel. She continued her journey home by air, pausing in turn in Luxor, Cairo, Jerusalem and Athens to visit the wonders of the ancient world.

Since September 1964 Margaret has been teaching Classics at King Edward VI Grammar School for Girls, at Handsworth, near Birmingham, and she is now the Deputy Headmistress. Although she leads a tremendously busy life, she has found time to learn Russian and is now able to teach it at evening classes. Last summer she went on a month's course to Moscow, which was organized through the British Council.

In the school holidays she loves to travel as much as possible, and her favourite countries are Greece, Norway, Austria and Switzerland. Sometimes she takes school parties abroad, and at other times she goes off on rambling expeditions amongst the mountains which were always her favourite milieu.

When Anne left the WRNS in the autumn of 1945, she returned with great joy to her home in Surrey, and to her horses which had always been her first love. She spent a great deal of her time on horseback, and she soon became interested in dressage amongst other things.

Some while later when she had settled in a home of her own in the hamlet of Farley Green, not far from Guildford, she started a stud of Welsh mountain ponies which soon became famous. Her stallions Coed Coch Cilcain and Coed Coch Peilat are champion harness ponies and are sires of many fine foals. They are both well-known prize-winners in the Private Driving Classes which are such a popular feature of horse-shows today. Altogether this pair of ponies have won more than forty first prizes in horse-shows, and the walls of their stables are liberally adorned with a colourful array of rosettes. To give some idea of their prowess, in 1966 one of the ponies won the Black Magic Championship at the Royal International Horse-Show, the following year the pair won the Pair Class and Championship at the last Richmond Royal Horse-Show, and in 1969 they won no less than twelve first prizes as well as the Reserve Championship at the Royal International Horse-Show. It seems a far cry from the day when we drove a pony and trap around the New Forest during our last twenty four hour leave before D-Day.

Anne is a member of the British Driving Society, which was founded by her cousin, Mr Sanders Watney, to foster the renewed interest in the driving of horses and ponies. She is its area commissioner for Surrey and Sussex, a member of the BDS Council and also of its Federation Equestre International Committee; she is also an active member of various other famous societies in the equestrian world, so that I would not be at all surprised to see Anne and her lively pair appearing on the scene at the next Olympic Games.

Finally Anne is a member of the Hurtwood Control which administers the beautiful countryside in which she lives. Altogether she leads a very interesting and active life, and when she takes an occasional well-deserved holiday, her favourite country to visit is Greece.

Sue left the WRNS in the late autumn of 1945, and after spending a few weeks at home with her mother in Micheldever, she started a year's course in cookery and floral arrangements at the Cordon Bleu. She gained a certificate at the end of the year, and her cooking has rivalled the art of Boulestin and Escoffier ever since that time.

In 1947 Sue, Winkle and I took a job together as deck-hands on a 100-ton Bermudian-rigged cutter called *Moonbeam* which was setting off on a two year's voyage to the Mediterranean. In actual fact the job only lasted for a few months owing to unforeseen circumstances, but it was a powerful experience which made a lasting impression on us all.

When Sue returned from this voyage, she worked as a Housemistress at St. Swithun's School in Winchester for a short while, and eventually she left this job to get married.

Since then she has lived in Micheldever and then in Winchester, and she now has four children, three girls and a boy. Her eldest girl has recently started her first job in Southampton, just as Sue did herself in that remote world we lived in around the time of D-Day.

Some years ago Sue took a course in china restoration, and from time to time she has been able to take advantage of this to mend, quite invisibly, the most delicate and beautiful pieces of china.

The family now live in a large house on a hill overlooking Winchester, with a stream running through the garden, and as Sue loves nothing better than to have the house full of children and young people, she leads a very busy life amidst a serene and cheerful atmosphere.

Of the five points on the star, Winkle has, perhaps, had the most varied career of all. After she was first demobbed she took a job in some pony stables near Exmoor. A few months later she broke her collar-bone whilst out riding one day, and had to return home to recover from this unfortunate accident.

Her next job was on a boat which was being converted for a long voyage in Tarbert, Argyllshire, but as the boat never left harbour and the plans for her departure were somewhat vague, Winkle left after a short while to join the *Moonbeam* with Sue and I.

She returned to England from this episode in September, 1947, and took a job at Burroughs Wellcome and Co. in Beckenham for about a year. This was a terrible experience as far as she was concerned, as she had to look after rabbits which were used for scientific experiments and she could not bear to be surrounded by so many sick and dying animals.

Her next job was as a filing clerk in the National Cash Register Company in Marylebone, and as she did not care for this much either, she came to work as a clerical assistant at the School Care Committee Office (London County Council) in Islington in 1949. I was also working there at the time, as a Care Committee Secretary for various schools in the area.

Winkle stayed in the Islington office for four and a half years, and then her great dream in life, which was to become a ballet-dancer, began to materialize. From the end of 1953 onwards she danced in pantomimes, summer shows and any other dancing jobs she could get, in many different parts of England. Often she had to do other work as well, in the evenings or in between shows, in order to make ends meet.

After a few years of this sort of life, Winkle began a three-year course at the Sigurd Leeder School of Modern Dance, working in a Wimpy Bar in the evenings for some months, and then as an X-ray filing clerk at the Royal Free Hospital. Some two years later her mother died, and there were so many complications to be sorted out over her old home in South Norwood, that she was unable to finish the course.

Her next job was a clerical one in a school near her home, and then followed a few months in the Youth Service Office at Clapham Junction. Finally Winkle decided to become a teacher, and she has been studying at a Teachers' Training College.

The world of dancing and the stage will always be her ideal existence, and despite the difficulties she has had to contend with, Winkle has passed a fair number of dancing exams. These include Elementary, Intermediate and Advanced Royal Academy of Dancing, two branches of the Associate Imperial Society of Teachers of Dancing, and she has gained two certificates connected with Dance Notation and an American form of dancing theory known as Labanotation.

Winkle also loves travelling, most of all to Russia where she can visit the finest schools of ballet in existence. Despite all her long hours of work and evening classes, she has managed to teach herself the rudiments of the Russian language.

As for me, when I left the WRNS at the end of 1945, I returned to my home in Sherwood Forest and did very little for the next eighteen months, apart from a course in Coastal Navigation, for which I managed to pass the final exam about a year later.

In the summer of 1947 I went with Sue and Winkle as a deck-hand aboard the 100-ton cutter *Moonbeam*, and when this job came to a premature end, I started working for the LCC in Islington as a School Care

Committee secretary for four schools in the area. Apart from the school holidays, I worked there five days a week for the next six years and part-time for a further eight years.

During the holidays I travelled through much of Europe, the Middle East and North Africa with my parents, and at the age of twenty-one I became the proud owner of a 22-foot converted ship's lifeboat called *Imp*.

Margaret Boggis came with me on our maiden voyage across the Channel in 1948, when we crossed from Dover to Dunkerque and navigated along the Belgian coast and through the Dutch canals as far as the Zuyder Zee and back in two hectic weeks' holiday. Each summer I continued to explore the coastline of Western Europe, sometimes with a friend and sometimes single-handed, until one memorable day in 1954 when the thirty-five year old Humber car engine with which the boat was fitted broke down in an onshore gale near the Belgian coast, and Winkle and I were cast ashore like pieces of driftwood. My beloved *Imp* was eventually towed into harbour by the Ostend Lifeboat, but she leaked like a sieve after her pounding on the beach and we had a rather perilous crossing back to Dover in her.

Soon after this episode I decided that it was time I learnt to sail, and in 1956 I bought my second boat, a 25-foot Folkboat which had won the East Anglian Offshore Championship the previous summer. With this boat, *Martha McGilda*, I have sailed many hundreds of miles in the past fourteen years, the two longest voyages being to the frontier between Russia and Finland in the Baltic in 1959, and to Western Norway, via six other countries, with my husband. in 1967.

I had my first article published in a magazine in 1960, and since then I have written for a number of newspapers and magazines, become a Fellow of the Royal Society of Arts and had my first book published in 1968.

I spent two years studying Serbo-Croat at evening classes in London, and I joined the Merchant Navy as an Assistant Purser on the car-ferry *Free Enterprise I* in 1963. I spent two very happy summer seasons in this job on the Dover to Calais run, and I gained a Lifeboatman's Certificate of Efficiency during my second season.

During a brief voyage to France in *Martha McGilda* in 1964, I met my ideal man, Dick Raynes, sailing on another Folkboat, and we were married a year later. We lived in the heart of the Kentish countryside for a year whilst he was working as a GP in Ashford, and then he started working for an East London Health Authority so we moved to Limehouse, where we now live in a very old house overlooking the River Thames.

A few of the other girls who worked at HMS *Gannet* still write every Christmas, two in particular; Diana Massey Bane, who married a New Zealander in command of one of the tank landing-craft during the war, and who has been living at Gisborne in New Zealand ever since; and Joan Scamell, who lived for many years with her husband and daughter on a splendid barge called *Plantagenet* on the Walton Backwaters. Joan is an active member of the Association of Wrens, and also a great friend of Tarzan, the Lowestoft fisherman whom everyone loved at HMS *Gannet*. He is now married and back at his old job again.

Harry McDade, the Scottish signalman on LCT 960, is another person who never fails to write each Christmas, and he and his wife and children have been living in the Lancashire cotton manufacturing town of Rochdale for a good many years now.

Last, but not least, I heard a rumour that Lt Sherwood was seen sailing into the harbour of Yarmouth, Isle of Wight, a few years ago, in command of a yacht manned by a crew of miniature Sherwoods whom he addressed in a manner reminiscent of the days of his wartime command!

And so the years flow by and the tides of human affairs ebb and flood, like the tides of the River Hamble in the long dark days before D-Day. Occasionally, when one or other of us is far away from the sea and feeling nostalgic for the days of our youth, we remember a verse from a poem of John Masefield's which has long been one of our favourites—

'A wind's in the heart of me, a fire's in my heels,
I am tired of brick and stones and rumbling wagon-wheels,
I hunger for the sea's edge, the limits of the land,
Where the wild old Atlantic is shouting on the sand.'

Limehouse, 1970

Me.

Winkle.

Rozelle and Imp (from The Sea Bird).

*Rozelle collecting car ferry tickets when working as a
Merchant Navy Purser (from* The Sea Bird).

Life Events

17 November 1925   Born Frederica Rozelle Ridgway Pierrepont, third child of Gervas Evelyn Pierrepont and Marie-Louise Roosevelt Butterfield.

29 August 1928   Older brother, Evelyn, died (aged 4).

21 February 1930   Older sister, Venetia, died (aged 9).

1940   Gervas Pierrepont succeeded his cousin to become 6th Earl Manvers. Family moved from London to Thoresby Hall, Nottinghamshire. Rozelle insisted on attending Queen Elizabeth Grammar School, Mansfield.

25 August 1943   Rozelle joined WRNS as 65152 Wren Stoker Pierrepont. Service included postings to HMS *Victory III* (drafting depot), HMS *Abatos*, HMS *Tormentor*, HMS *Squid*.

22 December 1945   Demobilised.

Summer 1946   Failed attempt to become yacht hand with friends Winkle and Sue.

November 1946   21st birthday. Parents assisted her to buy small motor boat named *Imp* in which she and her friends made cross-Channel voyages with mixed success. *Imp* was finally wrecked near Ostend 1954.

1953   Marries Major Alexander Beattie of Coldstream Guards. Divorced 1961.

1955   Father died. Rozelle inherited estates.

1956   Bought 25' Folkboat *Martha McGilda* from racing yachtsman Noel Jordan.

1959 Sailed *Martha McGilda* to Russia—mainly single handed. Invited to join Royal Cruising Club.

1963 Working as purser for Townsend Thoreson cross-Channel ferry *Free Enterprise*.

23 June 1965 Married GP Dr Dick Raynes.

1966 Rozelle and Dick sailed *Martha McGilda* to Norway.

1968 Publication of *North in a Nutshell*.

1971 Publication of *Maid Matelot*.

1974 Launch of *Roskilde*.

1975 Beginning of project with 8 boys in care of social services Edith Moorey House Newham.

1979 *The Sea Bird* (describing solo voyages with *Imp*, *Martha McGilda* and also her time as a purser).

1984 Death of mother.

1991 *The Tuesday Boys* (an account of the project teaching the 8 boys to sail).

1995 *27 Kisses: the Last Coach from Croatia* (an account of providing homes at Thoresby for 14 refugees from Croatia).

2001 *A Boat Called Martha*.

2006 *Limehouse Lil* (account of change in the docklands community. Includes purchase of *Beagle* and involvement with East Coast Sail Trust).

2008 *Memoirs of a Turkish Bear*.

3 January 2014 Death of Dick.

22 June 2015 Death of Rozelle.

An Appreciation

I T WAS MY privilege to have known Rozelle Raynes for the last twenty five years of her remarkable life. Sailing was our point of initial contact, shortly after she had moved her beautifully maintained Folkboat from the Thames to Walton-on-the-Naze on the Essex coast where I kept my own small smack-yacht. It was the sight of *Martha McGilda*, ghosting past my own *Kestrel* as I lay on my mooring that caught my eye, for FB 15 was a pretty sight and I was admiring her slipping out to sea in a light south westerly air.

Like Windermere in the Lake District and the Norfolk Broads, this was Arthur Ransome territory, the Walton Backwaters providing Ransome with the location for his children's novel *Secret Water* while the confluence of the Rivers Stour and Orwell a short distance to the north was the location of the beginning of *We Didn't Mean to Go to Sea*. And that warm afternoon as I fiddled with some small chore, *Martha McGilda* seemed to reflect this, for there was a clutch of boys in her cockpit presided over by a smiling skipper—Rozelle. As I read the name, beautifully painted on the little yacht's raked and varnished transom, I realised who this beaming lady was and that her crew were what I had come to know from her books as 'the Tuesday boys' from Rozelle's original weekly trips on the Thames with a crew of likely lads. However, that day was neither a Tuesday, nor did these boys hail from the East End of London. These details I learned later that sunny day, after the youthful crew had left *Martha* and I had come ashore from my mooring to walk round to her berth in the marina to make my number. As I had suspected, we had friends in common and within minutes I had been introduced to Rozelle's husband Dick and invited to enjoy a cup of tea. We were soon nattering about boats and books as if we were already the firm friends we soon afterwards became.

Rozelle—and Dick—were indeed wonderful friends, both to me but also to my family. Not having children of her own, she took great pleasure and interest in the company of those of others. Thereafter we regularly sailed in company, sometimes swapping crews and enjoying a pub dinner after a long day offshore. Besides these encounters we visited each other, and Dick and Rozelle were the most kind, thoughtful and generous of hosts to all who knew them.

In *Maid Matelot* Rozelle only hints at her aristocratic birth, showing a modesty that marked her character. When her father, an earl, had told her it was time she went to a private ladies' academy she refused point-blank and went instead to the local grammar school situated, as she would have said, 'on the outskirts of Sherwood Forest'. I have a vague memory of her telling me how she hated 'coming out' as a debutante, as was the practice for young women of her background in the 1950s, and she makes plain in this book how she hated the dances she was supposed to attend as a young socialite. Sadly she lost both her siblings, so grew up a very single-minded young woman, bucking the social norms of her upbringing and finding in boats and the sea that solace for the soul that made her a true romantic.

It is clear from the part of her life that she records here that the years she spent as a WRNS Stoker were deliriously happy and led—eventually—to her acquisition of *Martha McGilda*. Her enthusiasm for polishing brass boat-fittings far exceeded my own, but we shared a deep affection for our respective boats, the magic of our cruising ground and a love for the simple satisfactions of small voyages. Moreover, she was always keen to remind me that, like me, she too had for a time served in the Merchant Navy, being proud to have become a competent 'lifeboatman' during her time as an Assistant Purser in cross-Channel ferries.

Her philanthropy was wide-ranging and that essential part of it—taking those disadvantaged and often troubled teenage boys to sea to give them a grounding in sailing and seamanship—became a minor legend among the yachting world of the Thames Estuary. She could not rescue all of them from their sometimes tragic back-grounds—I well recall her grief when one of her original 'Tuesday boys' was later murdered—but she was joyous in the successes of others and proud, never of her own part, but of theirs, on finding that stability that leads a young man to some form of self-fulfilment.

The part of Rozelle's life that she recalls here in Maid Matelot is more than the celebration of a young woman's early encounter with small boats and the milieu in which she would take great delight throughout her long and worthy life; it is also an illuminating record of a vital part of the Second World War, the build-up to the sea-borne invasion of Europe on D-Day, 6th June 1944, and the weeks of reinforcement that followed. All this filled her with a characteristic enthusiasm, her zest for life near tidal water shining from almost every page.

She wrote several books, many illustrated with her own drawings (an ability inherited from her mother, Countess Manvers being a prolific and talented artist) most of which convey a sense of her delight in and enthusiasm for life. She bore bravely the failing eyesight of her last years as well as the loss of her beloved Dick, and at her death, in July 2015 aged 89, was mourned by many.

All-in-all, as I remarked earlier, it was a privilege to have known her and I am pleased to have been asked to pay this rather inadequate tribute to a great and indeed noble lady.

Richard Woodman

Richard Woodman is an Elder Brother of Trinity House. He began his career in the Merchant Navy, then spent thirty years with Trinity House. He is a novelist and historian.

Martha McGilda *(from* The Tuesday Boys*)*.

Index

Micky outside HMS *Gannet*.

Maritime Titles from Golden Duck

The Yachtsman Volunteers Collection:
- *The Cruise of Naromis: August in the Baltic 1939*
  GA Jones (with an introduction & afterword by Julia Jones)
- *Man the Ropes: the Autobiography of Augustine Courtauld—Explorer, Naval Officer, Yachtsman*
  Augustine Courtauld (with an introduction by Susie Hamilton)
- *From Pole to Pole: the Life of Quintin Riley*
  Jonathon Riley (with a foreword by Noël Riley)
- *Maid Matelot: Adventures of a Wren Stoker in World War Two*
  Rozelle Raynes (with a foreword by Hugh Matheson and an appreciation by Richard Woodman)
- *We Fought Them in Gunboats* (HMS *Beehive* edition) (forthcoming)
  Robert Hichens

You may also be interested in *Uncommon Courage: The Yachtsman Volunteers of World War II* by Julia Jones, published by Adlard Coles, additionally available as an audiobook.

The East Coast:
- *The Deben* (biannual magazine)
  River Deben Association
- *Waldringfield: A Suffolk Village beside the River Deben*
  Waldringfield History Group

We also sell Robert Simper's books on East Coast history, people, and boats.

The Strong Winds Series by Julia Jones (with illustrations by Claudia Myatt):
1 *The Salt-Stained Book* (available as an audiobook)
2 *A Ravelled Flag*
3 *Ghosting Home*
4 *The Lion of Sole Bay*
5 *Black Waters*
6 *Pebble*
7 *Voyage North* (forthcoming 2022)

Books by Claudia Myatt:
- *Anglo-Saxon Inspirations: Designs to Colour and Create*
- *Keeping a Sketchbook Diary* (new edition forthcoming 2023)
- *One Line at a Time: Why Drawing Is Good for You and How to Do It*
- *Sketchbook Sailor*

We hold most titles in Claudia Myatt's RYA *Go Sailing!* series.

For a full list of Golden Duck titles, including the Allingham family series, *Wild Wood* by Jan Needle and the *Please Tell Me* activity books for older people, see golden-duck.co.uk. Most are additionally available as ebooks.